Interviev

Christine Ingham

FOURTH ESTATE • *London*

Christine Ingham is a full-time writer on careers and employment. A former secondary-school teacher, she has published several books and previously set up an employment project with the Rathbone Society.

Also by the author

In this series
Jobfinder

Life Without Work
Working Well at Home
New Work Options
101 Ways to Start Your Own Business

First published in Great Britain in 1997 by
Fourth Estate Limited
6 Salem Road
London W2 4BU

Copyright © 1997 Fourth Estate Ltd

10 9 8 7 6 5 4 3 2 1

The right of Christine Ingham to be identified as the author of this work has been asserted by her in accordance with the Copyright, Designs and Patents Act 1988.

A catalogue record for this book is available from the British Library.
ISBN 1-85702-627-6

Typeset by York House Typographic Ltd, London
Printed in Great Britain by Clays Ltd, St Ives plc, Bungay, Suffolk

Contents

Acknowledgements

I gratefully acknowledge the assistance of all the individuals and organisations without whose help this book would be less than complete, including the City University Business Library, Coca-Cola GB, the Co-operative Bank, the DfEE, the Institute of Personnel and Development and Reed Personnel Services plc.

Introduction

The job market is a mobile place. The demand for skills has changed; job security is more fragile and 'regular' employment is simply less regular. Few people will have a job for life. For most, working life will consist of several stages with different employers, whose only common feature may well be the interview process at the outset.

Competition for jobs can be intense, and a good honours degree or a professional qualification alone will not guarantee success. This book considers what employers want and what they look for at interview. It also examines the way in which large and medium-sized companies are refining their selection procedures, and how to prepare for interview. Many employers are using increasingly rigorous selection techniques to try to reduce the high costs incurred when an unsuccessful appointment is made. This means that, in an already competitive job market, unprepared candidates will be even more likely to fail at interview.

Many of us will be applying for jobs more frequently than in the past, whether through choice or because of the growing prevalence of contract work. Once you have embarked on the selection process, the job interview is the final, make-or-break hurdle.

Overcoming the competition and meeting recruiters' expectations at this stage demands interview skills of a high order. It means making the best of what you have, knowing how to promote yourself at interview, and making sure you have the facts at your disposal to make an informed decision about whether to accept a job offer.

Some people shine naturally at interview; most of us have to work at it. But interview technique can be developed by improving skills, body language, confidence and the ability to handle awkward questions. In presenting a picture of how interviews operate and what employers want, *Interviews* offers a crucial advantage.

1 Them and Us

Rejections are demoralising and stressful. Being invited for an interview can be exhilarating and confidence-boosting, but it also brings anxiety. Familiar questions cross every candidate's mind. Will I be able to answer all the questions? Will I be able to answer any questions? Will I make a fool of myself?

Few spare a thought for the difficult task facing the interviewer. Although the job interview remains the most widely used method of selection, this is 'despite its limitations as a reliable predictor of future job performance', according to the Recruitment Code of the Institute of Personnel and Development.

Research has indicated startling shortcomings in the job interview process (see Eder and Ferris, 1989). Studies of interviewers have concluded that most perform poorly in terms of how they make decisions and how they structure and conduct interviews with candidates for jobs. An interviewer who is about to make life-changing decisions on your behalf may not necessarily know what she is doing.

THEM

Demystifying the aura which surrounds the many and varied people who call themselves interviewers will help you place both the interview and the interviewer in perspective.

THEIR AGENDA

Finding someone to fill a vacancy is only part of the interviewer's agenda. Interviewers, like candidates, bring to an interview their own personal and professional concerns and biases, only some of which they will be aware of. Whatever an interviewer brings into the interview room runs the risk of affecting her performance, judgement and decision.

Studies carried out in the 1980s (for example Smith and Robertson, 1989) showed that interviewers have unconscious preferences for candidates who are attractive, assertive and similar to themselves. It is therefore important to pay attention to dress and presentation, to prepare well and to practise for the interview so that confident answers happen by design rather than by accident.

It is also useful to find out as much as you can about the interviewer. Interviewers unconsciously – and consciously – respond more positively to candidates whom they identify as belonging to the same 'group'. For example, if your age, sex, race or background is different from the interviewer's, she may place you in a 'not similar to me' category. In these circumstances, concentrate on establishing and playing on other 'similar to me' points of reference. These may include attitude, manner of speech, education – even body language (see Chapter 2).

Performance-related pressures from the interviewer's line manager can find their way into an interview room. W.H. Smith estimates the cost of recruiting and retaining a new member of staff at around £2,500. The financial implications of recruiting the wrong person are bound to be on the agenda of interviewers in any organisation.

The interviewer may also worry about having to report back to a senior member of staff on the interview procedure. Her own job or promotion may be on the line.

She may be anxious about the implications of falling foul of employment legislation; it could be the first hiring decision she has had to make; or she could have financial, family or other worries unconnected with the interview.

Interviewers also know they have to do a certain amount of selling of the job and the company to the candidate. Although the level of unemployment may suggest that the balance of recruiting power is still in the hands of employers, interviewers have to try to hire the most able and suitable person to fill a vacancy, and that person may have other job offers. The right candidate has to be attracted.

The only potential solution to the problems faced by the interviewer is the interviewee. Whatever else she may have on her agenda, it is worth remembering that when she calls you to interview, an employer is saying: 'I want to meet you. I am interested in you.'

WHAT THEY LOOK FOR

Employers want to appoint people with more than the basic technical capacity to carry out the tasks in the job description, and the interview is designed to show more than basic professional competence. A 1996 study by one of the big employment agencies, Reed Personnel Services, indicates a growing realisation that 'human qualities are as important as technical skills in the current competitive work environment'.

Reed Personnel's study of 220 organisations revealed a growing emphasis on teamwork. 'Interviews allow you to get a feel for personality and whether someone will work with existing staff,' was a typical remark from one employer.

This is borne out by Coca-Cola's Human Resources Director for Northwest Europe, Bernard Kunerth. When asked what puts one candidate ahead of another at interview, he too mentioned interpersonal skills. It is important to be a team player, not a solo player, and to be able to transfer and share knowledge with colleagues.

Research into graduate-selection interviews, carried out by Neil Anderson and Viv Shackleton at the University of Sheffield in 1990, showed that 'the suitable graduate was perceived as interesting, relaxed, strong, successful, active, mature, enthusiastic, sensitive, pleasant, honest and dominant.' British Telecom's graduate-recruitment interviews assess personal attributes during the first of a two-stage recruitment process, along with the candidates' background, track record and motivation.

A candidate's motivation is a key point to many employers. Along with social skills, it is often cited as one of the main criteria by which employers judge the people they interview (Landy and Trumbo, 1980). If you can demonstrate that you are keen to work for the company and that you have the right motivation for the job, you are half way there. Conversely, a first-class degree will count for nothing if an employer suspects the motivation is missing.

Motivation is difficult to assess from an application form, though application letters can give some indication. The interview is the best forum for candidates to show an employer how keen they are. Equally, if you are half-hearted about the job or the company, there is every likelihood this will come across. Genuine enthusiasm is difficult to fake.

People new to the job market who are applying for trainee management posts can score points by demonstrating leadership qualities, initiative, and social and interpersonal skills, according to a paper presented to the British Educational Research Association Conference. But what is seen as most important depends on the type of job. Appearance is more important to recruiters interviewing for sales positions, while co-operativeness and physical well-being are more important when interviewing for unskilled work.

Since almost a third of people end up working for small companies rather than multinationals, it is important to understand what employers in these businesses look for. Research carried out at the University of Hull (Bartram et al, 1995) into the recruitment of first-jobbers by small businesses revealed 'a strong emphasis by employers on the importance of personality characteristics – such as honesty and integrity – and of interest in the job (motivation). All were rated as far more important than ability, aptitude or attainment.' If you know what they want, it is easier to deliver at interview. It seems that qualifications are less important to this group of employers than enthusiasm and approachability.

INTERVIEWERS

The professionals
Most interviews for posts within large organisations are carried out by trained professionals who – by and large – know

how to conduct an interview, ask the right questions and base judgements on facts, not subjective impressions. This sort of interviewer will ensure the interview is structured and run well, which is particularly important if there is more than one interviewer. She will ask questions based on the job description and person specification (sent out to candidates) to help her identify those who match her selection criteria. Decisions about each interviewee will be based on factual evidence given in his replies. This is in accordance with the Institute of Personnel and Development's Recruitment Code, which states that an interview provides the opportunity to gather additional information and 'to assess the suitability of candidates against a job and person specification'.

Blue-chip companies know how important it is for their recruiters to avoid subjective assessments and bias. British Telecom trains all its recruiters in interview skills, stressing that interviews should be used 'to build up evidence rather than impressions'. When BT recruiters meet applicants they are alert to sweeping generalisations about 'masses of experience' and unsubstantiated declarations of intent.

Research by Eder and Ferris shows that structured interviews with professional, trained interviewers, when questions are focused on job-related criteria, are fairly good at identifying the right person for the job – though they are not infallible.

The amateurs

The unstructured, 'informal' interview, run by someone with little or no training in interview techniques, compares unfavourably. However well an interviewer knows her company or department and its work, this is no guarantee that she knows how to conduct an interview well enough to find the best person to fill a vacancy. She may well be unaware of the influence of her personal preferences and biases in her hiring decisions, which all too frequently means she offers the job to someone who may not be the best candidate.

I once had such an 'informal' interview with the director of a small company with a dozen staff. He began with some small-talk about life, the weather and cricket, and I listened, nodding at what I hoped were appropriate points. The chat continued, so after a while I began to venture occasional comments: 'Who'd have thought he'd be out for a duck?' and so on.

And so it went on. Eventually I began to suspect it was a test of initiative to see whether I would be able to wrest control of the conversation from him. I steered the conversation round to the job interview. More than an hour later I left, wondering what the point of our meeting had been. If you apply for a job in any of the creative fields, this could happen to you.

There is never a guarantee that the person who interviews you is good at it, even if she has been trained in selection procedures and techniques. It is also worth remembering that interviewers are human. They may even be more nervous than you; they may have slept badly, or not had time to prepare properly because of other work pressures; they may feel slightly threatened by an impressive CV.

Neither the interview process nor the interviewer is infallible. If an interview leaves you feeling confused, angry or frustrated, it may be because the interviewer did not know how to conduct it.

A well-run interview should:

- be organised efficiently. There should be no sudden interruptions to fetch notes or chase staff who are supposed to be present. There should be proper instructions and an outline of the ground which the interview intends to cover

- address questions related to a job description and a person specification (of which you should have been given copies), and be conducted by interviewers who are seeking facts about your ability to do the job, not amassing subjective impressions

- provide you with the opportunity to give full answers and to ask questions

- be run by interviewers who acknowledge that interviews

are stressful for candidates and try to put them at their ease.

Conversely, signs of a badly run interview include:

◆ disorganisation

◆ superficial, irrelevant, confusing, badly-worded or unfocused questions

◆ a rushed interview or an inattentive interviewer

◆ indications that personal bias overrules evidence of ability to do the job

◆ an interviewer who plays power games on unsuspecting candidates.

US

PERSONAL AGENDAS

Just as interviewers have concerns beyond the simple desire to fill a vacancy, so do candidates. It is worth examining our personal agendas to assess whether they might affect our performance at interview, and if so to take the necessary measures.

Although few people relish the prospect of an interview, it should be seen as the forum for a professional exchange of information in which both parties try to assess whether a positive match exists between us, the job and them.

Our personal agenda is what prevents us from approaching the interview as a calm, focused exchange of information. Some of the following pre-interview anxieties may ring a bell:

Reactions to authority figures

You may react to interviewers with rebelliousness or fear; you may see them as quasi-parental figures. Projecting past conditioned responses on to interviewers interferes with the process of entering into a genuine dialogue. Unfortunately, you may not realise that you are reacting this way.

The need to please
The desire to be liked interferes with straightforward inter-actions. Giving the answer you think interviewers want to hear will cause problems in the long term if it does not reflect what you really think. At the root of this concern is the fear that if you dare to be yourself you run the risk of rejection. It is a sign of lack of confidence.

Personal biases
The interviewer has them. No doubt, so do we all. But the verbal interaction and the facts provide the real basis on which to judge the job, the company and its prospects.

Passing the test
It is not unusual to see the interview as a test. Memories of previous tests – driving tests, or final exams – can be a barrier to seeing the interview as a forum for a professional exchange of information.

Other fears
These are legion. You may suffer from fear of the unknown, fear of letting your family or others down, fear of the competition, fear of imminent financial pressures, and so on.

The more anxieties you can overcome, the better. They will not help the interview. The first step is to acknowledge your worries; the next is to face up to them before the interview. Discussing them with someone else almost always helps.

Positive issues
Do not forget that there are also positive issues on the agenda. The more they are allowed to come to the fore, the better.

Motivation
If you feel highly motivated about a job it will tend to show at interview – if you let it. When interviewers meet a candidate who appears highly motivated, and whose responses reinforce

this perception, they will mark him up. If you feel enthusiastic about a job, do not be afraid to let it show.

Keenness to work for the company

If you are invited to interview by a company you particularly admire, again, do not be afraid to let your enthusiasm show at interview. Complimentary observations about the company can help. Let them know it is their particular company you want to work for, and be ready to explain why: for example, they are the market leaders in their field; they are at the forefront of new developments; they are known for providing the best service or products.

Knowledge of your field

Your knowledge of a particular field relating to the job is a big advantage. Keep this in mind, and let it bolster your confidence. If you have the skills to do the job, the interview is the place to display the extent of your knowledge.

Knowledge about you

You alone have complete knowledge of your professional self. The interviewer's aim is to gain access to this information, which puts you in a powerful position. Make the most of it, and be prepared to feed edited highlights to the interviewer.

The interview spotlight

While some people may enter an interview looking for the opportunity to shine, most of us are reluctant self-publicists. We shy away from the interview spotlight and are inclined to give minimal responses to interviewers' questions. Yet the interview is a candidate's opportunity to reveal his best points and ensure the interviewers understand why they should offer him a job.

WHAT WE LOOK FOR

An interview is also an opportunity for you to find out more about the job, the company, and your prospective employers, managers and colleagues. It is a two-way assessment, though this can prove difficult if you find yourself facing an interviewer who is not skilled at directing the proceedings. You may have to steer the interview in the right direction to acquire the information you need.

An interview should be seen as simply a means of exchanging relevant information between two parties. It is a meeting of professionals whose shared goal is to assess whether the person is right for the job and the job right for the person.

Success in Four Minutes or Less

A job interview typically lasts anything up to forty-five minutes, but it appears that the length of an interview may, in reality, be academic. Why? Because researchers both in Canada and at Aston University in the UK have shown that interviewers make their minds up about a candidate's personality within just the first four minutes of an interview. Other experts reckon it takes only 120 seconds – not long by anyone's standards. So perhaps we should forget about the length of the interview for a moment and concentrate on how to make the best use of those crucial first few minutes – on how to make the right sort of impression. Psychologists call it 'impression management'.

IMPRESSION MANAGEMENT

The term refers to 'conscious or unconscious attempts to control the images that are projected in . . . social interactions' (Schlenker, 1980). And if there are only four minutes in which to do this at interview, it's important to look at how a good impression might be managed in those few decisive moments. According to Reed Personnel, a common remark made by employers is 'Above all, it's the first impression that counts.'

The right sort of impact at the start of an interview is a central factor in making a success of it. This isn't just a commonly held belief. Findings by researchers at Sheffield University confirm that those of us most likely to succeed are the people who are most skilled at impression management.

What is rather disconcerting about this in the interview

situation is that interviewers normally do all the talking in the first few minutes. They introduce themselves and show the candidate where to sit; they settle down and shuffle papers, which takes up a few more seconds; and then they normally chat about the job and the ground they intend to cover. Often all candidates have said by this stage is 'Hello' or 'Good morning/afternoon' and one or two 'Thank you's – if we are lucky. Not a word about qualifications for the job, not even time to utter experience's first syllable. So it is hardly likely to be the brilliance of our conversation which informs those important first impressions.

NON-VERBAL SIGNALS

Since we have so little chance to speak in the opening four minutes, body language – non-verbal behaviour, all those silent messages which we send out intentionally or which slip through in a split second by accident – is left to do the talking for us. Our body language creates the first impression as firmly as if it had been set in concrete and steel plate. Whatever comes afterwards is used only to verify the initial judgement; anything which does not conform tends to be ignored or manipulated until it fits.

Psychology professor Albert Mehrabian looked at what it is that makes the strongest impression on the people we meet. He found that our impact depends only 7 per cent on what we actually say, 38 per cent on how we say the words and use our voice but over half, 55 per cent, on the unspoken signals we transmit. The Professor of Communication at the University of Pennsylvania, Ray Birdwhistell, considers the figure even higher. He reckons that almost two-thirds of our interaction during a conversation is at the non-verbal level.

All this is not to imply that the answers we eventually get around to giving after the first four minutes aren't of any importance. They are. In fact research carried out in the USA into non-verbal signals during selection interviews showed that 'High levels of non-verbal behaviour had a more positive effect than did low levels only when the verbal content was good.' So micro-signals can only be of help to us at interview if we also manage to answer questions well. In fact, if we become past masters at managing our 'non-verbals' but give poor responses to questions, positive body language can actually work against us. In the words of the researcher Keith Rasmussen, 'When verbal content was poor, high non-verbal behaviour resulted in lower ratings.'

So both the answers we give and the non-verbal messages we send are important, one complementing the other. If the competition is tough and we are running neck and neck with another candidate, Rasmussen believes it is the quality of the 'non-verbals' which can swing the decision one way or the other: 'in interview situations in which all the applicants are of similar credentials and backgrounds, non-verbal behaviour has a relatively large impact on the final ratings'. So it would seem that we ignore how our body talks at our professional peril. Car manufacturer Toyota formally assesses body language during job interviews. It's a fair assumption that other employers do too, whether subconsciously or overtly and relatively objectively, as part of the formal interview procedure.

PHYSICAL MAKE-UP

Although we can tinker around with many aspects of our presentation – how we conduct ourselves and how we make use of our body language – there are some aspects which just simply are. Gender, size, race, age, attractiveness are elements that we can do nothing about – and nor should we. But they are obviously an integral part of the impression we make. The question is whether the effect works in our favour or not.

First the good news. Gender apparently has little or no effect on ratings at interview, according to researchers. This is also what is demanded by equal opportunities legislation. The law is on the side of anyone who thinks she might have been discriminated against because of gender. The same goes for race.

With regard to age the picture becomes more complex – and potentially more problematic. At present there is no legislation against employers who take a candidate's age into consideration in the recruitment process. So if you feel you have been discriminated against because of your age, there is precious little anyone can do about it. Whether it actually does count against someone at interview depends on the job, the interviewer and the company. For example, B & Q actively encourages and recruits older applicants. Other companies are less open-minded. An Employers' Forum on Age survey showed that unemployment among older workers doubled after the early 1990s. Women fare worse, with age discrimination kicking in after forty; with men it becomes more prevalent after fifty. Rather worryingly, a *Guardian* survey in October 1996 revealed that one in six people experience age discrimination even in their thirties. The gap between being 'too young and inexperienced' and too 'old and past it' appears to be narrowing at a furious rate among some – but, thankfully, not all – employers.

For those with disabilities employment law is changing – slowly. Before 1996 it was not against the law to discriminate against someone because of disability. Now, with the introduction of new legislation, it is, although employers can still reject someone if they think disability provides a good enough reason for them to do so. Also the new law applies only to businesses which employ twenty people or more, so those of us with disabilities may still find ourselves discriminated against by small businesses. Applying for jobs with larger companies and those with equal opportunities policies and good track records is perhaps the best bet.

Something which can't be legislated for, but which has also been studied by researchers over the years, is a candidate's attractiveness. Some say this does affect the outcome of interviews (Riggio and Throckmorton, 1988), while others say it matters only with certain jobs (Beehr and Gilmore, 1982). Since attractiveness is such a personal thing, it's not worth worrying too much about. Take comfort from the thought that Michelle Pfeiffer or Mel Gibson would fare worse in the interview than you unless their basic knowledge and qualifications to do the job were superior to yours. Making the best of whatever we have is all we can do – and, whatever that amounts to, at least impression management allows us to enhance what we have by other means.

ENTHUSIASM AND CONFIDENCE

Employers want to see enthusiasm in a candidate. As we saw in the previous chapter, motivation is one of the most desirable qualities as far as employers are concerned, particularly in younger applicants. Employers reason that skills, qualifications and ability can all be taught or acquired, but it is next to impossible (or, at the least, very hard) to motivate someone to do a job of work if enthusiasm isn't there in the first place.

Enthusiasm for the company and the job is a key weapon in anyone's impression-management armoury. Interviewers need to see we are interested. Asking questions at the right moment helps. So does offering additional information during the course of the interview, and responding openly when something of particular interest is said.

You may stumble over replies during the interview, but if you can show you are keen, many slips will be forgiven and forgotten. Enthusiasm alone will not get you the job, but it will certainly go a long way towards it. On one occasion when I was on an interviewing panel appointing a new manager the person who was offered the post was the one who managed to convey his absolute enthusiasm for his work. He talked relevantly about his commitment to community enterprise and about the projects he had got off the ground. On paper he was an outsider. In terms of experience with the intended client group he scored practically nil. Yet although some of the other candidates would have been fine in the post, we all felt he was the one we wanted to fill the vacancy.

If you feel enthusiasm, don't be frightened of letting it show naturally. You won't be believed if you go overboard and waffle on about how great everything is. Natural enthusiasm shows in how a person's face lights up and how their voice lifts and lightens spontaneously. That is enough to help convey your feelings.

Confidence is harder. Like enthusiasm, it is difficult to fake. When it's not genuine it can manifest as brashness, even arrogance – guaranteed to work against anyone at interview.

Yet even genuine confidence can suffer at the hands of interview nerves (more of how to cope with those in Chapter 5).

Posture and body language, which we'll look at next, can help project an image of self-confidence, as can presentation. But what about the real thing? Where does that sort of confidence come from? And how can we manage to project it in the first few minutes we have available to us at the start of an interview?

Psychologist and body-language expert Dr David Lewis believes, 'The surest way to make others form a bad judgement about you during the first four minutes is to feel badly about yourself.' In his book *The Secret Language of Success* he continues, 'Only by learning to love yourself will you ever be able to radiate the confidence, energy and enthusiasm needed to make a lasting and positive impression on others.' This tells us not to torture ourselves about any weaknesses we may have or any past failures we may have experienced. Instead we need to be kind and compassionate towards ourselves. Hand in hand with this goes accepting that it is reasonable to acknowledge to ourselves our strengths and past successes. If we don't, who will? This was illustrated by Dr Rebecca Curtis and Kim Miller at Adelphi University in the USA, whose work is mentioned in *The Secret Language of Success*. They found that 'If you feel good about yourself then you will tend to assume others will also like you. And if you believe you are likeable people are going to share that belief.'

When facing the prospect of an interview many of us fall into the trap of concentrating on self-doubt – not exactly the best way to generate self-confidence and definitely not part of good impression management. We should concentrate instead on what we are good at, what we can do, what we have accomplished. Cynthia Stevens and Amy Kristof, in their research at Maryland University, cite self-promotion and positive statements as key impression-management tactics. Other researchers, (for example, Kacmar *et al.*, 1992) have shown that such tactics elicit positive evaluations and hiring decisions in interviewers.

Confidence at interview comes from reminding and reassuring ourselves about what we can do and how well we fit the bill for the job we are going after. It comes from concentrating on the positive things we know about ourselves, not on the unknown prospect which faces us at interview. Confidence also comes from top-notch preparation – being forewarned and forearmed.

So confidence isn't something which can be slapped on like an extra splash of hair gel, otherwise it ends up looking just as unnatural. It requires:

◆ solid preparation

◆ reassuring yourself about all the positive points relevant to your application for the job: your skills, experience, qualifications, motivation and so on

◆ believing in yourself: as psychologist and philosopher William James said, 'The greatest discovery of my generation is that human beings can alter their lives by altering their attitudes of mind.'

BODY LANGUAGE

In our concern about what to say at interview, what to wear and all the rest, it's understandable if we pay scant attention to our body language. Yet we do ourselves a disservice to underestimate its importance at interview, especially since there is evidence that it can have a significant effect on the outcome.

Our body movements generally are relatively spontaneous, and in raising our awareness of what we do (or don't do) we run the risk of becoming awkwardly self-conscious. Still, it's worth considering and being aware of what works and what doesn't. If repeated failure at interview leaves you feeling confused about what you might be doing wrong, even after giving what you thought were good responses, slight improvements to your body language might hold the key.

THE EYES HAVE IT

Frequent eye contact is one aspect of non-verbal behaviour which has been found to go down well with interviewers and to create a good impression (Parsons and Liden, 1984) –

depending on how it's done. Staring fixedly at someone is interpreted as a sign of hostility. Avoiding all eye contact is worse.

Most of us aren't used to being the focus of the level of attention we receive during an interview. A form of escape from the discomfort of being under such intense scrutiny is made by breaking, or not making, direct eye contact. It is a mistake. Reed Personnel say that employers cite an inability to look someone in the eye as one of the major reasons for being put off a candidate. Some interviewers, like those at car makers Toyota, make a note of the level of eye contact candidates make, and other body language, during the recruitment process.

Researchers have shown that job applicants who maintain eye contact are judged by interviewers to be alert, assertive, dependable, confident and responsive and as having initiative (Amalfitano and Kalt, 1977). From their studies of graduate-selection interviews Neil Anderson and Viv Shackleton at the University of Sheffield go so far as to recommend that 'Interviewees would be well advised to maintain high levels of eye contact with the interviewer and to display frequent positive facial expressions so as to maximise their chances of success.'

Looking at people means you are paying attention to them and recognising their presence, thereby satisfying what American psychologist Abraham Maslow has identified as a basic need of all human beings. It's a simple way of giving someone a psychological hug – of saying you accept and like them. And most of us, being the responsive creatures that we are, tend to return the compliment. Interviewers are likely to say to themselves (subconsciously), 'This candidate obviously likes me, so I'm going to go right ahead and like them in return.' This is why averting your gaze can be so damaging in your dialogue with an interviewer.

SMILE, PLEASE

Next to eye contact, smiling is one of the other important non-verbal actions which say almost more to an interviewer than any smart answers he is likely to hear. A key ingredient in making a good impression during those crucial first four minutes is to smile warmly when you meet the person or people who will be interviewing you.

Facial scanning takes a triangular route from the eyes down to the mouth and back. Even when a candidate isn't speaking, an interviewer will be noticing their mouth. Beware of sticking a frozen smile on your lips, but do give a relaxed smile whenever appropriate.

HEAD FIRST

Not surprisingly, interviewers pay most attention to a person's face and head during an interview. And there is a lot they pick up from what they see there.

Researchers have identified nodding as going down really well with interviewers. This simple gesture is interpreted by them as an indication that you are listening to them and, just as important, it signals agreement. It is a good way to establish a sense of common ground and shared perspective, and it has been identified as positively affecting an interviewer's rating of candidates.

From experience I know it works. There's nothing more off-putting than having a glum, unresponsive individual to interview. Your heart sinks. Even allowing for nerves, some interviewees don't seem to appreciate that interviewers are human beings who look for some good, healthy, positive interaction, even though it is within the formal constraints of an interview. Trying to establish the sort of rapport which will enable a good exchange of information to take place between candidate and interviewer can be hard going.

Other head-related gestures:

- tilting the head slightly to one side reinforces that you are listening well to what the interviewer is saying

- tilting it back isn't such a good idea – it sends a defensive or arrogant message

- drooping the head forward slightly is associated with

non-assertiveness and/or a lack of confidence, which is exactly the opposite of what employers want to see

◆ biting or pursing lips or chewing the inside of your cheek are all nervous gestures, which work against creating an impression of relaxed, quiet confidence

POSTURE

The way people carry themselves says a lot. Since deportment is one of the first body-language signals interviewers read as you enter the room (and, remember, the majority will be doing so completely unconsciously – although this doesn't lessen the impact or importance of whatever they read), it is your first chance to transmit a positive message. Sagging shoulders speak of defeatism. Slouching implies that you don't care. Walk into the room upright but relaxed.

Posture continues to matter even when sitting. A well-supported position, with your shoulders square and sitting full back in the seat, will give the impression you are feeling relaxed and confident – just what an interviewer wants to see. I interviewed one candidate who perched right on the edge of the chair throughout. I kept feeling she was about to sprint out of the room; in turn, it put me on edge. However, occasionally leaning forward slightly when the interviewer is speaking gives the impression of inclining towards the job and the company, which reinforces the message that you're keen and interested, as well as paying the interviewer the compliment of showing that you are attentive to what they are saying. When ready to answer a question though, relax back again into the chair. These movements need to be made unobtrusively – candidates look odd when they keep bobbing purposefully backwards and forwards.

SIGNALS BY SEMAPHORE

We all tend to wave our arms around to a greater or lesser extent when explaining something or as we become involved in what we are saying. This is fine. It shows a certain amount of enthusiasm. What can work against someone in interview is not the occasional flourish but the sort of fidgeting which can be downright distracting to watch. If this is a problem for you when you are nervous, it may be worthwhile to practise sitting with your hands gently resting in your lap or on the arms of a chair. Folding your arms to try to control their waywardness, however, tends to look uncomfortable and hostile.

Whatever other movements you make, hands need to be kept away from touching the mouth, head or face. Experts say that when a hand flies up near to, or over, the mouth this implies a person is trying to hide something or signalling that the questioner has just touched upon a sensitive area.

How a person returns a handshake is used by some inter-viewers to assess character. A limp handshake will be interpreted as indicating a weak personality, an overly firm one as aggression. Ask friends to comment on your own handshake and practise responding to other people's hand-shakes.

A couple of final points about body language:

◆ it is important to curb fidgeting not just with your hands but with the rest of the body too, such as foot tapping, leg swinging, shuffling about in your seat and so on. If this is a problem, practice will help and so too will choosing a role model: an actor, a fictional character, a public figure or someone you know. Sit calmly *as if* you were this person

◆ other countries have different body-language signals and interpretations. If you are being interviewed abroad, you may want to check out if there are any special gestures to avoid

◆ learn to read body-language signals by watching how people interact in public places

◆ when people have struck up a rapport it is reflected through the natural mirroring of each other's body language movements. Use this to your advantage by occasionally and very subtly mirroring the interviewer's own movements. If they lean over to one side and you follow suit a few seconds later, it helps to create the important 'similar to me' effect, but do be careful with this – if done too obviously or frequently, it can back-fire

- finally, just as interviewers read candidates' body language, so candidates can read theirs. It pays to be aware of any helpful signals they send out unconsciously and to respond accordingly. For example, if they start to break eye contact, they may be signalling you are being too long-winded with an answer.

LISTENING SKILLS

Entering into a productive dialogue at interview requires more than producing a splurge of facts at the first possible opportunity or repeating statements about how well we think we fit the job. Good rapport is established first of all by showing the interviewer that we are listening. Body language can indicate to him he has your full attention, but good listening involves more than simply looking attentive.

Concentrating on what an interviewer actually says is vital. It is easy to be distracted by the new environment, by thoughts about prepared questions or by simple nervousness. It is not uncommon for attention to drift. As soon as this happens, active listening stops. Key points, indicators, subtle messages and meaning can all be missed while you're busy considering how to work into your replies something about your track record in sales. Good listening is 100 per cent listening.

Some interviewers make it difficult to listen well. They may ramble. Questions may be convoluted by anecdote. Their own nervousness or language skills may interfere. There may also be distractions from other panel members or noises outside the room.

If, for whatever reason, you do find you've missed part of a question, it is fine to ask an interviewer to repeat it (so long as this doesn't happen too often). If it is a matter simply of not understanding what she has said, it is also fine to say something like 'I'm not sure I understood the question', and she will probably rephrase it. On the other hand, if you are not sure whether you have got the gist of a question, it's reasonable to paraphrase what has been said to check your understanding before you give your reply. 'So what you want to know about is how I handled the drop in productivity?' Better this than answering inappropriately.

If you find active listening difficult, hone your skills beforehand by listening for about two minutes to a recording of the news or some other factual programme, then repeating or writing down what you heard. Play back the recording and check your accuracy.

IT'S NOT WHAT YOU SAY ...

We know from Albert Mehrabian's study that 55 per cent of communication is made up of silent speech signals (that is, non-verbal behaviour – the body language we have looked at). The next major factor in communication is not what we say but how we say it. This affects 38 per cent of understanding.

It has been suggested by researchers that 'A single well-executed self-promotion utterance may elicit higher survey ratings than ten poorly executed self-promoted utterances.' Delivery is more important than wordage.

I have yet to find anyone who has not been surprised when he first hears a recording of his own voice. It's an enlightening experience. Record yourself, and if you feel your delivery lacks punch, here are some pointers:

◆ quiet mumblings won't do much to impress an interviewer; be clear and precise

◆ a monotone implies a lack of spark and intellectual dullness; practise varying the ups and downs in your speech

- crisping up your consonants brings emphasis into speech and can help make replies sound more confident

- practise 'pointing', or emphasising, words in a sentence – helpful when wanting to make a more forceful delivery

- check the speed of your speech – too fast and the interviewer may not catch what you say, too slow and you may seem ponderous.

Much can be done to improve performance by making use of these various impression management techniques. They do work. Practise beforehand until new behaviours start to form a natural part of your repertoire of communication skills.

The Ground Work

Success at interview is as much to do with preparation as anything that takes place in the interview room itself. Good preparation shows. Coca-Cola's Director of Human Resources confirmed the truth behind this when asked about what is guaranteed to make a bad impression at interview: without hesitation he cited lack of preparation, including little or no knowledge of the specific job.

The aim of preparation isn't to trot out a few facts and figures or set answers in an effort to impress. In fact, doing so may have the opposite effect. Good preparation, on the other hand, tends to show naturally both in the way we handle ourselves generally during an interview and in how the factual content of our answers demonstrates the contribution we could make to both the job and the company as a whole. Hyperbole scores nil. And if you have been wondering how you can ever feel more confident at interview, sound preparation is probably the answer.

There are four areas of preparation and planning which will help to put you ahead of the competition: research, protocols, interview technique and questions.

RESEARCH

THE COMPANY

The amount of information sent out to candidates varies from one organisation to another. Generally the larger the business, the more likely that information will be made available to job applicants. This may be sent out as an application pack to initial enquirers, or it may be reserved for those who make it to the interview short list.

Typically, at its most basic, it will contain a brochure about the company (which may be little more than a leaflet) and a job description (which may contain no more information than appeared in the advertisement). Clearly this won't provide much more insight than you have already. But even a mass of material, although useful, won't help put you ahead of the competition as it will have been sent to all other candidates as well.

However much or little information you are sent, digest it thoroughly. If at interview it is apparent you have not read even the most basic information about a company, you won't be offered a job by them. Andy Hutchinson, Recruitment Manager for the Civil Aviation Authority, says that whether candidates have made use of the literature sent out by the organisation is a fair indication of their level of motivation. From his perspective, if you cannot be bothered to read what they send, you are not really that interested in either the job or the company. On the other hand, candidates who show they have not only read the information sent to them but have also taken the time and trouble to find out more are bound to come across as highly motivated.

Encyclopaedic knowledge of each company which invites you to interview isn't the aim – if nothing else, there will probably not be the time to amass and digest it all. So the following list of suggestions is meant to serve only as a springboard for research and to start you thinking of useful matters to find out about, depending on the company you're applying to and the type of job for which you're being interviewed. The list isn't meant to be exhaustive or inclusive.

You may want to look into:

◆ their full range of products or services

◆ company size, present growth pattern and history

◆ profitability and any recent changes either up or down

- specific employment policies

- major customers/suppliers in UK, Europe and beyond

- job/department/branch-specific activities (for example, recent marketing campaigns)

- any major reorganisations

- recent press coverage

- major new contracts

- information about key figures in the company, including whether you have a membership or other interest in common

- main competitors and their present activities

- local presence: community activities, sponsorships, etc.

- any recent awards

- sensitive areas (for example, bad press coverage)

- corporate-specific jargon

- values the company espouses

- whether they are part of a conglomerate.

Besides using the literature sent to you by the company, other sources for unearthing additional and more detailed information include:

- annual reports and sales literature – just phone, tell them you'll shortly be attending an interview with the company and ask them to forward copies of the material you need

- newspapers – local, national broadsheets (especially the business sections), specialist magazines and trade press

- people – who work for the company or know someone who does, who work for one of their competitors, who work in the same business sector

- recruitment staff – Jobcentres, careers offices, employment agencies, careers staff at colleges/schools

- Internet

- CD-Roms (libraries) – business/company information, newspapers on disk

- directories (libraries) – for company, product and services information (for example *Kelly's Directory*).

PRE-INTERVIEW VISITS

Pre-interview visits may not be compulsory, but it is not unusual for invitations to be couched in phrases like 'We encourage all prospective applicants to attend.' Is it worth it? The undoubted answer is yes. What you see will help you work out how to demonstrate at interview your suitability for the job and organisational fit.

It is also worth bearing in mind that even though there may be powerful and genuine reasons not to go, an employer might interpret your decision not to attend as indicative of a lack of real interest and motivation. If there is a problem with the day and/or time they suggest, phone them up to enquire whether it would be possible to attend on another day.

A visit might include:

- a tour of the premises

- a visit to the department or section where the successful applicant will work on a day-to-day basis

- a presentation (possibly using film, video or multi-media) about the company, including the work of the department, section or branch to which candidates are applying

- an introduction to the managing director and/or line manager

- a chance to meet a member of staff from Personnel

- the opportunity to talk to previous new recruits and/or staff who would be your work colleagues

- a look at any specialist equipment or technology which a successful applicant would operate

- a tour of staff facilities, like the canteen or on-site sports facilities

- a general behind-the-scenes look at the company and what it does

- the opportunity to see their full range of products

- a chance to see a production line or process in operation.

Do bear in mind that anything you are shown will inevitably contain a certain amount of company hype and commercial propaganda.

While you are being guided around, ask yourself some of the following questions:

- is the atmosphere calm or chaotic?

- have staff personalised their work stations?

- do staff look pressurised?

- are any awards, press cuttings or information about pending launches on display? These bits of information could prove useful at interview

- what about evidence of community involvement?

- are staff friendly – with each other, with you as a visitor and with customers?

- what does the interaction between senior staff and those in the lower echelons tell you about management–employee relations?

- what do noticeboards tell you? Are they covered with prohibitions from management or posters encouraging staff to sign up for training courses or join in with social activities?

In addition, take advantage of the chance to ask questions and find out more about what the job demands. Questions might be:

- the throughput of work – are there peaks and troughs or is it pretty steady?

- how is the workflow controlled? Try to get a feeling about whether the workload is reasonable

- how much time is spent in meetings? With whom? To what purpose?

- what are the *real* hours of work?

- how many people work in the department/section?

- what do they enjoy most about the job?

◆ what do they enjoy least about the job? They are unlikely to tell you that the job is mind-numbing even if it is, but they may bring to your attention an aspect which you had not considered

◆ which aspect of the job demands most of their time?

If an invitation to a pre-interview visit has not been extended, it may be worth contacting the employer to ask whether something can be arranged. Sue Bland of the Co-operative Bank says this not only shows an applicant has initiative but also is a good indication of how keen and serious they are about the job.

The information you glean will help to confirm whether this is the company for you. Assuming the company inspires your enthusiasm, any information you have will help you anticipate a little better some of the veiled agendas of the person or people who will be interviewing you. You will be better prepared to gauge where they're coming from.

Whatever you find out will add to your knowledge of the selection criteria for the job you're after. A job or person specification details only what they are looking for as it relates to the job of work itself; it will contain nothing about the fact that the company has just won a contract with a firm with which you have had previous dealings, for example, or an award for community involvement – just the sort of thing you were interested in at your last place of work. Think about how you might demonstrate at interview an awareness of these company issues and any clear matches which exist between the company's concerns and your own skills, experience, abilities and work interests.

Proving you will fit into the company's broader picture is important. Most businesses are anxious to find candidates who will make what has been termed a good 'organisational fit'. Most have had painful experience of the difficulties inherent in employing someone who may have the right skills but turns out to be a company misfit.

All companies have certain values and attitudes. A good fit will be noted if you can demonstrate that you share them. If customer care and environmental awareness are at the top of their agenda, you need to know it – and to show that you have the same concerns. For example, if you belong to Friends of the Earth *and* wrote a dissertation at university on the importance of customer-care training, let them know at the appropriate points. If the company has a positive mind-set, as is the case with a company like Coca-Cola, then you need to demonstrate through your answers that you are the sort of person who sees opportunities rather than problems and that you also like to make things happen. Tell them about how you made positive use of the six months you spent while unemployed and how you set up sponsorship deals to launch the college football team on a Europe-wide tour. Whatever their company culture is, you will increase your chances of a job offer if your answers reflect a good match between yourself and the organisation you are applying to.

Demonstrating that you would fit in well will help to reassure them they would be making a good decision if they offered you the post. Unless you can supply evidence yourself that a good organisational fit exists, the company will have to gamble on whether you will enhance the running of the business. Valuable information comes their way when they are given evidence of a good candidate–company match. And if two candidates are running neck and neck for a job, this may be one of the things which swings the job offer.

PROTOCOLS

A crucial aspect of good preparation is knowing what to expect so that we don't (a) make an obvious gaffe or (b) get totally fazed by what happens or what we're expected to do.

Because interviews are quite formal affairs, even when they are described by the employers who hold them as 'informal', they have their own set of rules and social niceties. Anarchic tendencies are best left at home if securing a job offer is a serious goal.

Some of these points will seem obvious, some even petty, but they are all established rituals in the job-interview courtship. Observing them demonstrates at a very basic level that you know how to fit in and play the game. If employers see that you are comfortable with the routine, they in turn will feel comfortable.

WHILE WAITING IN RECEPTION

◆ sit quietly with your thoughts or browse through any company literature that may be there

◆ be polite to reception staff but not familiar. The impression you make on them may not be a planned part of the interview process, but feedback could affect an interviewer's decisions.

THE INTERVIEW ROOM

◆ knock before you walk in; don't hover around outside waiting to be called

◆ close the door behind you

◆ approach the interviewer, but wait to be invited to sit down

◆ let them take the initiative about handshakes

◆ they will lead the conversation, so don't feel tempted to launch in

◆ if there is more than one interviewer, each one will be introduced to you (try to remember their names). Again let them take the initiative about handshakes, otherwise just smile and nod as each introduction is made.

PROCEDURE

◆ the interviewer will probably ask some innocuous question about whether you found your way there all right.

This is not a trick question but small-talk to make verbal contact and put both of you at ease

- they may describe how the interview is to progress and what they intend to ask you about

- the first few minutes may include information-giving about the company and/or job. This brief time could provide last-minute clues about what questions to ask later on

- when they have concluded their questioning they will normally ask if you have any questions. This is the point at which to mention areas which may not have been covered, as well as to ask prepared questions.

CLOSURE

- they will probably tell you about the decision-making schedule and when you can expect to be notified

- they will thank you for coming in and probably offer a handshake, although it is best still to let them take the initiative

- say simply, 'Thank you for seeing me'

- don't be tempted to say anything more once this stage has been reached – leave and close the door behind you.

GENERAL

- don't smoke while you wait

- always address interviewers by their surname, even if they include their first names when they introduce themselves

- don't be too liberal with your language; slang and swearing – however idiomatic or effective – are inappropriate

- looking at your watch is tactless and suggests boredom.

The conventions of interviews may not seem interesting or important. They are not. They exist only because it will be easier to hold a useful conversation if both parties have some shared expectations about the pattern of the interview. It is not in our interests wilfully to ignore these – they are the means to an end: the job.

INTERVIEW TECHNIQUE

A good interview technique is partly acquired (the more interviews you attend, the better you get) but can also be learned. A lot hangs on honing those all-important communication skills, both verbal and non-verbal, that we looked at in the previous chapter and form part and parcel of a person's impression management. In addition we'll consider a few tactics which work.

TOP AND TAILS

A night-club singer revealed the secret of how to leave an audience with the impression that they have just witnessed an all-round good performance even though that may not be the truth. She noticed that if she made sure her opening number hit the spot, and then made equally sure she went out with a blast, whatever went on in between didn't matter too much. All that people remembered about the show afterwards is that it started and finished brilliantly, conveniently forgetting the rest.

Politicians experience something similar. Those in power promise their all at the beginning of their term in office and use that period to build up the electorate's hopes; towards the end of the term they suddenly become reinvigorated. Everything in between they put down to mid-term blues – which they know voters will forget about when it comes to putting their cross in the right box again.

In the context of interviews, psychologists refer to this as the 'primacy-recency' effect. An interviewer will tend to recall best what happens at the beginning of an interview (including those vital first four minutes) and at the end. Bear this in mind if an interview seems to go badly in the middle – or even if it doesn't. An interviewer is likely to be left with the impression of having witnessed a good performance if the top and tail of it are handled well.

SELF-PROMOTION

Self-promotion simply means stating the facts – without even the slightest hint of over-statement – about how you see yourself, your future plans and your past achievements. If this feels uncomfortable, consider what you say as providing additional factual material to help the interviewer make the right choice. If experience, in or out of the work environment, has uncovered leadership skills, a potential employer would probably like to hear about it. If you have previously set, worked towards and achieved certain goals and targets, talk about them. And, while you're at it, tell the interviewer about the problems you encountered and overcame along the way.

This interview skill has been shown to affect positively employers' perceptions of applicants for a job. Give them the facts, but don't tell them how wonderful you are. Go back through your CV and cast your mind back over situations in which you achieved certain things, discovered new aspects about yourself or met new challenges. Be honest. Lay rightful claim to your accomplishments. In the job market little can be gained, and much lost, by hiding one's light – but do leave all empty, unjustified claims under the nearest bushel.

PHRASING ANSWERS

'Well, the scheme ran for quite a while and I suppose you could say I sort of helped to let people know it was there.'

Compare that statement with this: 'The scheme ran for two years. I helped to raise its public profile by getting the local press to run regular articles on us.'

The first sounds hesitant and unfocused. An interviewer isn't interested in whether the scheme ran for one or two months either side of two years, and by the time she or he has waded through the padding in your answer, any little impact it might have had will have evaporated. By comparison, the second is dynamic and focused, and it asserts the interviewee's involvement.

Think clearly, and polish the way you answer questions. If you're not sure how you come across, record yourself in a question-and-answer session with a friend. It can be about anything (but may as well be a mock job interview). The important thing is to listen to how you phrase replies and to practise sharpening them up. Concise replies convey assertiveness and confidence – both very popular with interviewers.

GENERAL DOS

◆ always tell the truth; leave the embellishments for when you are having a drink with friends

◆ let the interviewer finish speaking – interrupting is out

◆ in the meeting of minds that is the interview, you may well stumble upon an area of disagreement. Arguing may win you the point but will almost certainly lose you the job. Better to acknowledge the employer's view and then move on ('I take your point' or 'I see what you mean')

◆ practise giving concise (but not abrupt) answers. Keep to the point

◆ keep answers focused on what you can bring to the job and company

- back up answers and claims with facts and examples. If you say you are good at figures, give evidence of this straight away

- make sure you know yourself inside out. The mind has a propensity for turning blank at interview, so you need to have all the relevant data to hand almost without having to think. Rehearse your strengths (and weaknesses), key achievements, experience, personal qualities, management and personal skills, qualifications, etc., and how these relate directly to the job you are applying for; be completely familiar with what you have said in your CV or application form

- know the key points which you want the interview to cover. Be prepared to mention them yourself. For example, you might say, 'I had hoped we would talk about my involvement with database management,' or 'I wanted to highlight my experience in telecoms.' Interviewers are human and can overlook topics or forget to ask questions they may have intended to ask

- go with the flow. If the interviewer says in passing something which catches your attention and which you could make use of, comment on it in your reply: 'I noticed you mentioned plans to expand into Europe. I'm very much interested in the European market and would like to see myself working abroad at some time in the future.'

It takes practice to make interview techniques work. Get friends to put you through your paces. If at all possible, video-record sessions so that you can see exactly how you come across, body language and all. It is only through seeing and hearing yourself objectively that you will identify areas that may be letting you down. It is also a good way of monitoring progress as you introduce new techniques into your repertoire of interview skills.

It may be worth finding out whether the local college, university, careers service or Jobcentre runs interview-skills training courses; if courses are not available, these organisations may at least help you set up mock interviews.

QUESTIONS, QUESTIONS

There are plenty of questions at interview – and some of them should come from us. At the end of interviews it is standard practice to enquire whether we have any questions we would like to ask. Have them ready. If we fail to come straight back with prepared questions but instead cast around vaguely only to alight on the idea of asking about something like holiday entitlement, our interest in the job will be marked down. 'I prefer to see an excess of curiosity,' observed one top employer.

But time is limited, so prepare just two or three questions (allowing for the fact that at least one might be addressed during the course of the interview). Use the company literature, information gleaned from research and the job and/or person specification to formulate questions.

- ask open-ended questions (those which require more than just a yes or no reply)

- avoid questions about perks, time off, entitlements, etc.

- avoid trivial questions, like 'Will I have a locker?'

- don't try to impress the interviewer with difficult, awkward or controversial questions. It won't work.

Appropriate topics for questions include:

- the company itself

- the future plans for the company

- the relevant department

- employment terms and conditions

- training opportunities

- job prospects

- anything which was brought to your attention during the interview.

Bear in mind an old saying which goes along the lines of 'Know the wisdom of a man by the questions he asks.' What you ask is not just a way of showing you know how to play by the rules of the game. Use this valuable opportunity to enhance the final impression which you leave with the interviewer.

Preparing Your Interview Kit

We've looked at some of the in-depth research and preparation which can pay dividends when you get to an interview. This chapter will cover some of the more down-to-earth, but no less important, aspects of preparing yourself. These include dress, appearance, travel and what might loosely be described as your interview kit.

DRESS

What we wear to a job interview is important: how we dress impacts on the overall impression created. As those first few minutes at the start of an interview – from the moment we enter the room – are so crucial, outfits must enhance the immediate impression and not detract from it. To ensure that happens, some thought and preparation have to go into deciding which outfit to wear and how to wear it.

Researchers in Canada have shown that there is a link between how candidates see themselves and the way they dress. They found that candidates who perceive themselves as highly motivated and socially poised dress more formally. In turn, this affects how the interviewer sees them. Although it doesn't make them think candidates are necessarily more highly motivated, the research shows they see the more formally dressed applicants as having more social skills – the basis of the job interview.

Other researchers have found that interviewers give a better rating to women who wear 'business-like' clothes: suits with dark colours, tailoring, heavier fabrics, and straight lines.

Of course, the selection of what and what not to wear depends on the type of job being applied for, as well as the company. This is where all that researched information will help again.

It's worth reading through the company literature once more, and noting the type of language used to describe the company culture. If they choose words like 'bright', 'go-ahead', 'enterprising', their dress code will differ from a company which prefers words like 'established', 'traditional' or 'stable'. How they describe their clientele or customers is also a give-away. Note the photographs that illustrate staff and work environment, and consider the overall design of the company literature. Is it sophisticated or 'safe'? Would you use 'Marks and Spencer' to describe the design or would you say it was more 'Vivienne Westwood'?

These pointers reflect the company culture and give valuable clues about how they expect their staff to dress. If you can get a feel for this, it will help to make the choice of what to wear that much easier; it will clarify what image would not look out of place. Remember, anything which helps suggest a 'similar-to-me' and organisational-fit effect at interview works in your favour.

Dressing appropriately is the key, but there are some general ground rules about dress code which are pretty universal:

◆ if it's about to fall apart, or if it's unclean or unpressed, don't wear it. Fix it or choose something else

◆ any hint of casualness will be seen by interviewers as a lack of care about the interview and an indication that the same attitude would be brought to work

◆ interviewers will not be looking for designer labels on your clothes – and many won't notice or recognise them even if they are there. Smartness is important; price tags aren't.

WOMEN

◆ bare legs, even with a tan, are best avoided unless the interview is informal

- avoid ostentatious jewellery

- make sure your outfit is one you feel comfortable in, especially when sitting

- jackets and skirts with a simple shirt or top are best.

MEN

- bare legs at interview don't look any better on men; wear plain, calf-length socks – and 'plain' doesn't include white, ever

- jackets, shirts and ties are still the norm for most interviews at the professional level unless you have good reason to believe otherwise

- avoid jewellery apart from a wedding or signet ring and a watch

- clear pockets of any bulk.

Although there is no suggestion that everyone going for a job should turn themselves into an interview clone, it is worth bearing in mind that how you dress is interpreted as a reflection of your ability to perform well at interview, your attitude and your state of mind. Interviewers will be more comfortable with, and will form a more positive impression of, candidates who, while still retaining their own sense of style:

- look as if they will fit in

- are smart and have made an effort

- are dressed appropriately.

APPEARANCE

From a short distance two things which can ruin the effect of an otherwise good outfit and professional appearance are hair and shoes. What may pass undetected during the initial sizing-up process is bound to be spotted during the next twenty to forty-five minutes when the interviewer's gaze rests squarely on us.

Interviewers often have their own personal hates, like dirty fingernails, dandruff on the collar or grimy spectacle lenses. Covering all bases is the only safe option.

HAIR

- keep your hair trimmed – you may get only a few days' notice before the interview; the same goes for beards

- if in the slightest doubt about whether you should wash your hair again for the interview, DO

- keep collars clear of dandruff and loose hair.

SHOES

- a new pair of shoes isn't strictly necessary, but the ones you have must be in good repair

- wear a new pair of tights – and have a spare pair with you.

PERSONAL

- bathe or shower beforehand so that you feel fresh

- do use an anti-perspirant deodorant, even if you don't usually perspire

- carry a clean, ironed and folded handkerchief

- avoid garlic and spicy meals and excessive amounts of alcohol the night before

- studies have shown that perfume and aftershave can negatively prejudice interviewers' ratings; play on the safe side and go very, very easy on them.

GENERAL

- ◆ the impression you are trying to create is one of organised efficiency: don't bring your notes in a plastic
  carrier bag

- ◆ carry as few things as possible into the interview room;
  leave newspaper, umbrella, coat etc., with the receptionist or in the car, or tuck what you can into your
  briefcase

- ◆ if you carry a mobile phone, remember to switch it off

- ◆ carrying a briefcase and handbag together can cause
  problems; try to eliminate one or other (preferably the
  handbag).

Knowing your overall appearance is up to scratch boosts
confidence. Interviewers' reactions aside, most people feel
better when they are well turned out. For further reassurance,
ask someone else to give your appearance an honest
appraisal.

TRAVEL

If the first four minutes of the interview are the most crucial
for creating the right impression, consider what impression is
created if a candidate isn't there at all during that time.
Interviewers, primed and waiting, make use of the first minute
to check over the application form of the candidate they are
expecting. They shuffle their papers around a bit. Four or five
minutes pass and irritation sets in because late-comers put
back their whole schedule. Finally they may decide to keep to
schedule, and if the candidate eventually appears they will give
him or her whatever time remains. It may be no more than five
minutes.

Absence creates the most vivid impression in the minds of
interviewers. A less than warm greeting when you finally

present yourself, breathless and dishevelled, is almost certain. It is fair to say that being late for an interview can be disastrous.

Having said that, accidents do happen; breakdowns occur; grid-lock is not unknown. Should you find yourself running late, it is absolutely vital to phone ahead and give some indication, if possible, of when you may be expected.

Getting the travel arrangements sorted out so that you arrive in good time, with ten or fifteen minutes to spare, is essential. The aim should be to arrive with enough time to find your way to the right office, section or department and to compose yourself, so that your image is that of an efficient, organised professional.

Details of how to get to the interview should have been included with the letter of invitation. Do check it over carefully. Double-check the address where the interview is being held (this may be different from the one on the letterhead). Double-check the time of the interview. It is not unknown for 12.30 p.m. to be read as 2.30 p.m. – and the error discovered too late. Also double-check where you should report on your arrival.

If information was not sent to you, phone the company and ask the receptionist, Personnel Department or secretary to send details. (Don't trouble the person who will be interviewing you for this information.) A small company may not have printed information, in which case take the details over the phone. Beware: if they say something like their office is just a 'short walk' from the nearest bus stop, check whether they mean a five-minute short walk or a twenty-minute short walk.

Obviously travel arrangements are a lot simpler if the interview is with a local company. You will already be familiar with bus, tube or train routes and with its general location. But to minimise the risk of being late, here are some pointers to bear in mind:

- ◆ if you do not know the company, check out the size of its premises – finding your way around a large site, especially if there is more than one building, will take time

- make sure you understand the location – if the company is on a large industrial estate or commercial/technology park, this will add time to your journey

- check with the bus or train company for times – and double-check the one you need isn't a peak-time-only service

- if driving or cycling, phone beforehand to check on parking availability

- allow for parking time, especially in built-up areas or if the company has a large car park

- have the number of a taxi firm with you

If in any doubt about the journey, do a dry run. It is worth the effort. Much can turn on whether travel arrangements run smoothly.

YOUR INTERVIEW KIT

Here's a quick suggestion list cum memory-jogger about what you might want to take with you. If you are forgetful, write a list of last-minute items and stick it somewhere where you won't miss it. Other items can be assembled the day before. Have ready:

- anything which the company has asked you to bring, like certificates, completed forms or work samples

- a copy of your application form and/or CV

- a spare copy of your CV

- map, address and telephone number of your destination

- the name of the person who will be interviewing you

- pen and small notebook or personal organiser

- small diary or pocket calendar

- a list of the questions you want to ask (try to memorise this)

- the job advertisement plus any literature you have been sent such as a job description – you may need to refer to it

- record of achievement, if appropriate

- money for parking meters/telephones/taxis

- spare pair of tights.

One's balance can easily be thrown by last-minute hitches. Preparation is the only way to militate against them, and even then things can still go awry. Take the time to organise yourself and cover the main points as best you can; that is about as much as any of us can do.

Interview Nerves

We all have nerves. But not everyone manages them equally well. For some of us, the stomach turns over; a cold sweat breaks out; feelings of edginess destroy any semblance of outward calm. Others may find themselves invigorated, even inspired, by some nervous anticipation. They may perform better thanks to the nervous energy. Control of that energy is the key. This chapter looks at various strategies for channelling nervous energy so that it becomes productive, and at some ways of calming it when it threatens to jeopardise all the effort that has gone into securing the interview.

The prospect of a job interview is often daunting, especially if we feel out of practice or if our previous experience at interview has not been successful. Compounding the stress are the personal hopes and dreams associated with each job application. A lot can depend on the outcome of an interview, which in itself creates more tension.

The good news is that a certain amount of stress is necessary at interview. Nervous energy helps us perform better. Without it an applicant can look so laid back she fails to convey enough enthusiasm or interest in the job. As the Co-operative Bank's recruiters say, interviewers often prefer to see nerves in a candidate. A problem arises only if nerves get out of control and threaten to undermine our performance.

FEARS AND REASSURANCES

Interviews provide a fertile hunting-ground for nameless fears to manifest themselves. Putting a name to those fears often helps. Think about whether any of these hit the spot.

FEAR OF THE UNKNOWN

If we can't actually see what there is to be frightened about, we tend to assume that whatever lies in wait is a hundred times more terrible than it actually is. This anticipatory anxiety, when related to job interviews, decreases with experience as it becomes obvious that they are not set up with the specific intention of humiliating us.

What stands on the other side of any interview-room door is an opportunity to demonstrate to a willing audience your suitability for a post; a chance to talk about your experience and skills and how they match up with what is demanded of the job being applied for. Whoever is waiting behind that closed door, you can guarantee one thing: they want to meet you.

FEAR OF FAILURE AND REJECTION

Out of the many interviewed (typically six or more), only one will be offered the job.

To put your fear of rejection into perspective:

♦ come to terms with the odds

♦ accept you can only do your best

♦ realise that employers are looking for a specific match not only between candidate and job criteria but also between candidate and their company culture. As Coca-Cola's Bernard Kunerth has pointed out, different companies have different cultures, and a candidate may succeed in one and not in another due simply to the degree of cultural fit. 'Failure' lies in a mis-match between you and the job. If employers do not see a good match, they could be doing you a favour in *not* offering you the job. Trust their judgement

♦ whatever the outcome, treat it as a learning experience to capitalise on in the next interview

And remember:

- if a job offer does not come out of this interview, there will be something better waiting for you further down the line.

FEAR OF RIDICULE

Catastrophic thinking can have the best of us imagining all sorts of disasters happening at the job interview, with us looking ridiculous in the eyes of the very people we are trying to impress. We worry about our minds going blank, exposing our weaknesses and generally making fools of ourselves. We begin to imagine that the interviewer's only abiding memory of us will be how stupid we were.

Again your own experience should eventually prove otherwise. Despite my own fears on this count as a candidate, I cannot recall any interview in which I felt that I had made as much of a fool of myself as I had imagined I would. And, as an interviewer I have seen people stumbling over sentences, misunderstanding questions and giving inappropriate replies. But in each case, when taken in the context of the interview as a whole, these mistakes have not dominated the course of the interview or determined whether a job offer was made.

It is not unusual for a candidate to fluff a question. Good interviewers will probe for a better answer and encourage a more thoughtful reply: they understand interview nerves and will make allowances.

WHAT HELPS?

PREPARATION

Key to helping to combat interview nerves is sound preparation. Without it we leave ourselves wide open to making fundamental errors: 'If only I had known beforehand they were moving into that market'; 'If only I had realised their new focus was on customer care'; 'If only I had bothered to find out their offices were so far away I wouldn't have been so late.'

After the event it is easy to see how more thorough preparation could have made the difference. And while the wisdom of hindsight can make a difference to the next interview, it can do nothing for the one just gone.

If you have done the research, by the time an interview arrives you should feel *au fait* with the company and its workings and ready for whatever may greet you. In addition, particularly valuable nuggets of information or knowledge will be worth their confidence-building weight in gold.

Getting there in plenty of time because you bothered to check out the travel arrangements beforehand and knowing you look your best are bound to help. And from the word go, as you call upon your knowledge of interview protocols and see yourself handling the situation with ease and aplomb, you won't have a chance to be nervous. Try to let the interview follow your plan. The questions too should be more or less what your preparation has told you to expect, and by the time it is your turn to ask questions you should be ready.

The armed forces know all about the value of preparation. Not only does it help to make operations run smoothly but it also ensures that each soldier feels confident about whatever he might encounter and doesn't fall prey to last-minute nerves. As interview candidates the value of preparation lies in knowing we are competent to deal with whatever we may encounter in the interview.

PRACTICE

Also key to overcoming nerves is practising your interview technique – and learning how to improve it. Chapter 2 looked at body language and communication skills, which are vitally important in helping to get the right message across. Practice in showing yourself at your best on those fronts will make the most of the answers you give. Chapters 7 and 8 look in detail at how to handle actual interview questions. Practising, preferably with someone to act as interviewer, and recording 'interviews' if at all possible will certainly help.

Like many companies, the Co-operative Bank has joined a new initiative launched by the Employment Service called Job

Preparation. This course enables long-term unemployed candidates to prepare for the selection event by providing training in interview techniques. If you are unemployed, it may be worth enquiring what is available locally through the Jobcentre or local Training and Enterprise Council (TEC). Contact numbers can be found in local telephone directories.

CALMING THE BODY

In focusing intently on what to say and how to say it, it is easy to overlook our physical needs in the course of preparation; yet if we do not feel on top physical form, we are unlikely to do ourselves justice. The state of our physical well-being can help or hinder at interview.

Here are some things to consider:

◆ interviews, and the build-up to them, are stressful. Since stress in itself makes extra demands of a body's resources, ensure your diet is adequate. Extra vitamin B and C supplements are recommended for helping the body's nervous and stress-response systems to cope

◆ watch how much coffee, cola and tea (to a lesser extent) you drink, especially on the day of the interview. Caffeine increases the amount of adrenalin in your blood – which is probably already higher than normal anyway

◆ avoid excess alcohol – a glass or two the night before won't do much harm, but a heavy drinking session the night before and any drinking immediately before the interview probably will

◆ a good way to burn off nervous energy is to do some exercise. This does not necessarily mean a full work-out – a good, brisk walk will do. Besides getting rid of any pent-up energy, it will also help clear the mind

◆ plan a relaxing evening the night before the interview.

Have an earlier night than normal only if you feel the need to catch up on some sleep; it is better to sleep well than to sleep long and fitfully.

RELAXATION STRATEGIES

Once nervous energy turns into stress it can be destructive. If stress is ignored, it can start to affect sleep and appetite, leaving us tired, irritable and as far from relaxed as we are likely to get. As an interview draws closer this is bound to affect performance on the day.

Sometimes sitting in front of the TV or having a drink with a friend is not enough to help achieve real relaxation. The shoulder muscles are still tense; the worried frown is still lurking.

Muscle relaxation

Trying to unbunch taut muscles can be difficult. One of the best ways is to work through the body from the toes upwards, first clenching each muscle group and then letting go. Follow the pattern of toes, calves, thighs, bottom, stomach, fingers, arms, shoulders, neck, face. Work through them, tensing each for a count of three, then releasing. Finally drop your tongue from the roof of your mouth; let it relax gently too. Take a deep breath and relax.

After going through the routine sit quietly for a few minutes with eyes closed, breathing gently.

Visualisation

This is a much used device to assist general relaxation. It requires the stressed person to visualise a particularly soothing image. The choice of image depends on the individual. One person may find the image of a still pool utterly calming, another the sense of floating gently through the air, another the sound of a gentle waterfall. Some may even find relaxation comes by imagining themselves in the interview – and succeeding.

Experiment to find an image which relaxes you. Whenever tension threatens to get the better of you, including just before the interview, close your eyes for a moment and concentrate on that image.

Affirmations

The use of affirmations helps to cut through the negative feelings and worry patterns which keep us feeling tense. Affirmations are positive statements, spoken in the present tense. They can help not only in putting a stop to anxious thoughts but also in giving reassuring messages to ourselves.

It is easy to invent your own. Just remember they must be in the present tense, simple and direct. Here are some examples:

- I am relaxed and confident

- I feel calm and at ease

- I feel positive and bright

- I am a strong candidate for the job

- I feel confident about myself

- I am well prepared and ready for the interview.

Say your affirmation over a few times to yourself or out loud (depending on where you are). Try to relax as you say the words. Concentrate on their real meaning; don't rattle through them without thinking – that will have little effect.

Use your affirmation(s) to reassure yourself about your candidature, your preparedness, your state of calm. The remarkable thing about affirmations is that even if you don't feel particularly 'positive and bright' or 'relaxed and confident' when you start saying them, you do by the time you have finished.

Pills and potions

If interview nerves are very bad, it is tempting to think about resorting to a tranquilliser or two. Although they quash nerves, however, tranquillisers quash all other responses too. It is worth considering alternatives which, while helping to calm the nerves, won't make you feel like a walking zombie. Many people find the following helpful:

- homeopathic remedies: aconite is helpful for stress, panic and extreme nerves and may have a beneficial effect on dire pre-job interview nerves. This remedy is available from most high-street chemists or health-food shops

- tissue salts: these small sugar pills, which dissolve in the mouth, work like homeopathic remedies. They are safe, non-toxic and non-habit-forming. Single tissue salts are available and are referred to by name, such as *kali mur*; combinations of two or more salts are referred to by a letter (combination B, for example, is for nervousness and edginess). Tissue salts are now widely available through most high-street chemists

- Bach flower remedies: these gentle remedies, made from flower essences, are said to be particularly useful for emotional problems. A few drops of the diluted liquid are taken up to four times a day. Cherry plum is for tension, fear and irrational thoughts; larch is for fear of failure and self-confidence; mimulus is for fear of known things; rock rose is for extreme fear and panic. There is also a combination called Rescue Remedy, which is helpful for restoring a sense of calm. These remedies are now widely available through leading high-street chemists

- herbal remedies: these too are now widely available. Remedies for nerves come in tablet form or as medicines, tinctures or herbal teas. Lemon balm is good for anxiety and makes a pleasant, relaxing drink. You might want to check out the new products which combine a number of herbs in tablet form, such as Kalms.

Aromatherapy oils

The sense of smell is powerful in evoking states of mind. Indeed, a thriving industry is based on it: the perfume industry. Aromatherapy oils use single extracts from plants, each one possessing different properties. Orange blossom is helpful for stress and panic; lavender oil is good for relaxation. Oils can be used in many ways, including in bath water or in a special burner. A few drops on a handkerchief can also be inhaled gently.

AT THE INTERVIEW

If, despite preparation, practice and relaxation the interview still brings on a bout of nerves, it is useful to have contingency plans as back-up.

One employer endorsed the acceptability of candidates taking notes or a copy of their CV into the interview. It is easy to be thrown momentarily by losing track of dates and forgetting which year was spent with which employer or by having your mind go blank when the opportunity to ask questions arrives. A quick glance at your CV or notes can help avoid this common problem. Check with the interviewer at the start that it is OK to use them.

If you start to lose the thread of the conversation, answer a question badly or stumble over your words, one of the best strategies is to admit to the interviewer that you are nervous – and, if necessary, say you would like to have another go at answering the question. This simple act works wonders and has the effect of restoring a sense of control as well as defusing the tension. A bonus is that good interviewers will, on hearing the admission, provide reassurance.

With a skilled interviewer, once the interview gets under way and a rapport is established between you both, self-consciousness and initial nerves tend to fade into the background. In any case, it may help to reflect that she may be feeling just as nervous as you.

Types of Interview

Nadia was applying for the post of assistant warden at a council-run nursing home. She filled out the application form and was delighted to receive a letter inviting her to interview. Details were given of the date, time and location; she was even provided with a map and told the name of the person she should ask for on her arrival, a Miss Rowley, the Head of Management. Understandably Nadia assumed this would be the person conducting the interview – or would it?

Looking more closely at the letter, Nadia identified three other names: that of the Personnel Manager, whose signature was on the bottom of the letter; a Miss Pratt, who should be asked for when telephoning; and, at the head of the letter, the name of the Director of Personnel. The letter gave no indication of what role they would play in the selection process and interview, if any; nor did it provide any information about the form the interview would take, apart from the fact that personality profiling would be carried out prior to the interview itself.

After thinking back over previous interviews Nadia drew on this experience and prepared herself to be interviewed by not one but two people: Miss Rowley, since she obviously had overall responsibility for the management of the council's homes, and the Personnel Manager who sent out the letter. As it turned out, she was indeed interviewed by Miss Rowley, but she was also interviewed by a Mr Johns, who was the principal warden, and by Miss Pratt, who turned out to be the personnel officer responsible for assistant warden appointments. Despite her experience Nadia was only partly correct in her assumption, but at least she was better prepared for what greeted her on the day than if she had stuck with her initial thought of being interviewed by one person – the one whom the letter directed her to ask for on arrival.

This is a common problem. Letters inviting candidates to interview do not always give a clear indication of who will be involved in the interview itself, even though other details are covered well enough. Psychologically this can put us at a real disadvantage. Expecting to be interviewed on a one-to-one basis only to discover a panel of six when the door to the interview room swings open is bound to affect our composure.

With this in mind it can help to consider what sort of interview to expect. Unless otherwise indicated, it's best not to assume that it will be just you and the interviewer.

ONE-TO-ONE INTERVIEWS

Among small businesses one-to-one interviews are by far the most common type of interview. The smaller the business, the more likely it is that it will be the owner, or 'boss', who conducts the proceedings. In larger organisations an interview may be conducted by the person who would be your line manager or someone from Personnel. Dave Bartram and his team's 1995 study of recruitment practices among small businesses when hiring young adults found that unskilled workers are more likely to undergo an interview with just one person than those who are being interviewed for clerical and semi-skilled or skilled work. The second group are more likely to find two people interviewing them.

The potential pitfall of the one-to-one situation is that it depends wholly on the capabilities, judgement and objectivity of one person. If that person is untrained and inexperienced, the interview they conduct may be very unsatisfactory. It is vulnerable to bias and whim, and it is in this environment that most interview errors are made. Much may depend on how well the two hit it off. In this sort of interview good body language and communication skills can pay dividends, so remember to show you are keen and give an animated performance.

The other situation in which a one-to-one interview can occur is when it forms one element of an extended selection procedure. More of this later (see pages 65–71).

PANEL INTERVIEWS

Consisting of more than one person, panel interviews (or selection boards, as they are sometimes called) are encountered more often in larger companies that are interviewing for skilled, clerical and higher-grade posts.

A panel can have as few as two interviewers and as many as six or more. Normally each person represents a particular aspect of the company with a vested interest in the appointment. In Nadia's case the interest groups represented were the department for which she would be working; the person with whom she would be working closely and who had a day-to-day working knowledge of what the job entailed; and the Personnel Department of the council, which would have a general interest in the appointment of a new member of staff joining the council's payroll and would ensure the council's recruitment policies were adhered to throughout the selection process.

Prior to an interview this sort of information is invaluable in helping you to anticipate questions, as each interviewer will tend to concentrate on his own specialist area. If you have not been informed who will be on the interviewing panel (or indeed whether there will be one), you might want to consider finding out. Do this when you phone to confirm you will be attending the interview. Explain that it would help in your preparation.

Although it may seem daunting to have to sit in front of what one may be tempted to think of as a firing squad, panel interviews can work in an interviewee's favour – if organised and run properly. The organisation is determined largely by the quality of the chairperson but also by the extent of the panel's preparation. If you doubt the chairperson's abilities, stay on your toes and do not allow yourself to be distracted by how poorly the proceedings are being run. Good communication skills and deft use of body language will help enormously. And if you suspect the panel is ill-prepared, your vigilance should make sure the key points about your application are covered. If you feel they have overlooked an important area, you can always raise it when they give you the opportunity.

Panel interviews, when run well, are often much fairer. The personal-bias trap to which one-to-one interviewers fall prey becomes modified when more than one set of opinions and observations have to be taken into account.

But a potential danger with panels is that members may be intimidated by one of the team, especially if that person is high up in the hierarchy. To disagree with him as he railroads his way through the decision-making process may be too risky in terms of whatever internal politics are in play at the time. Sometimes it is possible to identify the group bully (not necessarily the chair) by the way he handles the questions he asks, by other panel members' body language (such as eyes frequently darting towards a person as an anchor point) and how he presents himself with regard to his colleagues. This is a challenge. If he is not the chairperson, do turn to face him more fully when it is his turn to ask questions and smile warmly towards him. Maintain good eye contact. In fact, use all the natural body-language skills you have at your disposal (look again at Chapter 2). If you can make a good impression on the key decision-maker without fawning over him, he may swing his casting vote in your direction.

TELEPHONE INTERVIEWS

Time was when interviews over the telephone were associated with a distinct group of jobs, such as telesales or casual and unskilled work. However, major employers like the Nation-wide Building Society and NatWest Bank have started to recognise the benefits of using the telephone at the initial screening stage and not just for unskilled jobs. NatWest has introduced it into its graduate recruitment programme. Other employers are likely to follow suit.

Although these employers use it only as a short-listing device, with more in-depth, in-person interviewing taking place at a later date, it is obviously important for applicants to handle themselves well at this stage in order to progress to the next.

If a telephone interview is on the cards:

- ◆ make sure you prepare yourself as if you were to have an interview in person. They already have your basic details on the application form; this initial interview will be used to establish key competences needed for the job. The interviewer may also be looking out for evidence of your level of motivation

- ◆ keep copies of your CV and application form, details about the job and a notepad by the telephone, ready for the call

- ◆ practise the way you greet people over the phone

- ◆ when the interviewer is talking, help to sustain a dialogue by responding where appropriate

- ◆ practise your communication skills. With nothing other than the sound of your voice to go by, good intonation and clear expression are vitally important

- ◆ smiling 'shows' over the phone; use it appropriately to lift your conversation and create a feel-good impression in the person on the other end.

VIDEO INTERVIEWING

Video-conferencing tends to be associated with business networking, but leading employment agency Reed Personnel identified its potential to help them in recruitment. They have now set up a network of fourteen video-interviewing suites whereby potential candidates can be interviewed at one location by a Reed Personnel recruiter at another. These video links enable the employment agency to make the best use of a limited number of specialist recruiters to interview candidates across the country. This may catch on with other recruiters – and employers.

If you are the sort of person who freezes at the very mention of the word 'camera', practising in front of a camcorder at home will help (try to borrow or hire if you don't own one).

Here are a few pointers to bear in mind:

◆ sitting in front of a camera does not mean you have to act – just relax and be yourself

◆ speak in your normal way (deploying your improved communication skills, of course)

◆ although you will see the interviewer based in the other location on a monitor, make eye contact by looking at the camera, not the screen

◆ assume the camera is on *all the time* you are in the video interviewing suite and not just when the interview starts.

ASSESSMENT CENTRES

Aware of the limits of the single-interview approach, many employers use a multi-part interview procedure, especially when recruiting large numbers of new staff. This method of recruitment is referred to (somewhat confusingly) as an 'assessment centre'. A centre is an approach, not a physical place or suite of rooms. It is also sometimes referred to as a 'development centre' and in literature to applicants may be called the 'recruitment' or 'open' day. An Industrial Relations Services (IRS) survey in 1996 found that although only two out of every ten businesses (i.e. less than 200 employees) used assessment centres, 75 per cent of large employees (with more than 5000 staff) do make use of them in the selection process. The larger the employer, the more likely you are to encounter one.

Instead of candidates having to perform well enough to impress within the space of a half-hour interview, assessment centres take them through a number of different procedures.

This provides a better opportunity for both candidates and interviewers alike.

For the candidate, the pressure to give a single best performance is eased, and an overall assessment means that ground can perhaps be made up in one of the other interview settings if a blip occurs early on – although each session usually assesses distinct elements.

Another benefit for candidates is that you have the opportunity to get a real feel for the job. Practical exercises usually simulate important aspects of the sort of work you would be doing. As a result of having had a taste of things to come, you can assess whether the job and/or company is what you are looking for.

From the interviewer's point of view, different interview strategies enable a more rounded and accurate picture of each candidate to develop, which in turn is bound to improve the accuracy of her impressions. For example, someone may have brilliant manual or other skills but, when seen in a team-working exercise, is identified as lacking the necessary level of interpersonal skills. In short, she would be good at her work but hopeless to work with. In a relatively brief single interview it would be easy for this to go unnoticed.

Land Rover Vehicles, part of the Rover Group, dedicates a whole day to interviewing groups of about fifty candidates wanting to join the company as manufacturing associates. Their day's programme includes:

◆ an opening presentation

◆ a forty-five-minute interview with two interviewers, based on the candidate's application form

◆ a group of five or six manual tasks, overseen by two leading members of staff who work on the production line

◆ a written aptitude test, which enables interviewers to assess verbal, mechanical and numerical skills

- a personality questionnaire

- a teamwork exercise

- a medical

- a factory tour.

It is only after candidates have progressed through the whole day's activities that an overall assessment is made and a decision reached on whether they would make suitable employees.

If you are applying for desk-based or management positions you may have to take part in exercises which simulate aspects of those types of work. Here are some typical exercises:

WRITTEN EXERCISES

Just as manufacturing associates for Land Rover take part in manual tasks to assess whether they have the necessary skills for the work they would be expected to do, so some employers test applicants' clerical skills for jobs in administration. For example, candidates applying to join the Employment Service are given sample calculations to perform based on a claimant's eligibility for benefit. For jobs at higher levels applicants may have to demonstrate their understanding of information contained in a typical document.

IN-TRAY EXERCISE

The day-to-day reality of office-based work is that incoming paperwork which demands immediate attention is a continuous feature. The in-tray exercise puts candidates through their paces in dealing with a set amount of typical paperwork in a limited period. This may involve responding to phone messages, writing and sending faxes, dealing with interruptions, deciding which tasks can be delegated (and doing so), writing a letter and so on. The way each candidate manages to prioritise the work forms part of the assessment.

PSYCHOMETRIC ASSESSMENTS

'Psychometric tests are well proven – and they're here to stay,' according to the Institute of Personnel and Development's Policy Adviser, Angela Baron. 'Testing for generic skills like leadership, creativity and team skills is on the increase, especially with new graduate recruitment, and this sort of potential is harder to gauge simply from application forms, past experience, CVs and interviews.'

For employers, psychometric testing is a more reliable way to successfully identify the recruits they want. That's why they're here to stay. While some questionnaires used in the selection process will try to assess whether candidates have key competences, others (known as aptitude tests) are more concerned with identifying personal qualities, and to these there are no right or wrong answers. In this respect there is little or nothing to fear about completing any psychometric assessments which may be encountered. Despite this, many candidates – about a quarter in the recruiting experience of the Civil Aviation Authority, although other estimates put the figure as high as 40 per cent – opt out of the selection process at this stage and fail to turn up at the pre-arranged time.

According to figures from the Cranfield Centre for European Human Resources Management, 45 per cent of organisations regularly use aptitude tests in the selection process. Other figures suggest the number is as high as 70 per cent in companies with more than 1,000 employees, and 85 per cent was quoted in one 1994 survey conducted by the Institute of Personnel and Development. Although their use is less common among small businesses, there is a strong possibility you may encounter one in your search for a job if applying to larger companies, especially for management positions. As so many drop out, you will significantly increase your chances of success if you simply turn up on the day.

Different types of psychometric tests are used to assess:

- ◆ attainment – what you have learned or know. This is a better indication than a stream of qualifications – or lack of them

- aptitude – a person's ability to understand particular types of information or information presented in a specific way. For example, it may be important for candidates to be able to read and understand diagrams for a particular job. In this case a diagrammatic reasoning test may be given. Other types of test include verbal reasoning, numerical reasoning, abstract reasoning and so on

- personality – whether you are outgoing, caring, laidback, etc. These tests are used more often in management-level selection procedures than for lower-grade appointments

- values – an indication of whether your personal values are in keeping with the needs of the job and/or company ethos.

If you are really nervous about the prospect of taking a psychometric test, it does help to practise (and see Appendix A). Some employers even send out sample assessments to candidates in order to help them become familiar with what to expect.

ROLE-PLAY EXERCISES

It is next to impossible to assess realistically a person's ability to deal with others on a one-to-one basis simply by asking about it. With a role-play exercise candidates have the chance to demonstrate how they would actually deal with, say, a difficult customer or an unwilling subordinate. From an assessor's point of view, she can see the level of a candidate's interpersonal skills for herself instead of having to take his or her word for it.

GROUP EXERCISES

Since at some stage many jobs involve group work of one type or another, a group-work exercise may be included in the assessment centre. This may take the form of a leaderless discussion exercise, a role-play committee exercise or a problem-solving exercise where everyone works together to resolve a dilemma (which may have a practical element to it).

Depending on the nature of the position being applied for, interpersonal, leadership, negotiating and influencing skills are among the accomplishments which assessors monitor. Evidence of creative thinking and of the ability to give and receive criticism and demonstrations of any job-specific competences will also be noted, if relevant.

PRESENTATION EXERCISE

How you organise and communicate information to a group of people may be of great importance to the company you are applying to. If so, you may be required to give a short presentation, using information and materials provided.

OFF-DUTY TIME

If the assessment centre is residential and lasts more than one day, there will inevitably be time to socialise. There may also be informal group chats when candidates have the opportunity to meet an employee and ask him about the job or company. Although it may be stressed that these sessions do not form part of the assessment process, it is best to assume otherwise. I once played the part of current employee during a recruitment-day programme and was required to give feedback at the end of the session – even though the groups of applicants were under the impression they were simply sitting around having an informal talk with someone who knew what the job was about. Similarly it is best to assume that evening sessions are part of the assessment, so do turn up, and drink moderately. Watch what you say to interviewers or company representatives in the relaxed atmosphere of the time-off periods. It's easy to let out something which, in the cold light of day, you wish you hadn't.

Whichever type of interview is used by the company you are

applying to, whether an informal one-to-one or a two-day residential marathon, what is central to the outcome is the amount of preparation you put in beforehand. As well as providing you with both necessary and useful information, it will give you that all-important sense of preparedness – which will see you through whatever may lie in wait for you beyond the closed door of the interview room.

What Everyone Wants To Know

No one can know exactly what interviewers are going to ask, or on what they will focus their questioning, nor how they may word the questions, or the attitude they may strike. What we do know is what interviewers *in general* want to find out about us at interview. This chapter will look in detail at the topics interviewers cover and the sorts of questions they may ask in the process.

It is worth recapping for a moment what interviewers want to establish:

- can you do the job? Do you have the necessary skills, experience and/or qualifications?

- do you want to do the job? What is your motivation for the job in question and/or the company? Do you really want this particular job or is it just a stop-gap? Do your personal work-based preferences (including salary expectations) fit the job?

- will you fit? Will your personal qualities and attitude match the needs of the job (such as flexibility or leadership), the work-group dynamics and the company culture (such as a positive attitude or respect for traditional values)?

Depending on the company and the job, an employer may look for evidence of potential at interview, as is the case with Coca-Cola, which focuses on the long term when interviewing candidates. In companies like this, the interviewer will include questions relating not only to the position being applied for but also to personal ambitions and latent qualities which could be developed and, later, brought to the fore. Such companies see a new recruit as an investment in the future success of their business. It is not just today they are interested in but tomorrow as well. The question for them is: do you fit into the longer-term picture?

With untrained and less able interviewers who conduct 'informal' interviews, the focus may well be less acute. They may be more concerned with 'getting to know you' and 'seeing what you're like'. Some may take it as read that you will be able to do the job just because you have the right paper qualifications, or they may have interpreted your CV in a way that satisfies them you could do it. Instead of targeting questions to establish real evidence of your ability to carry out the functions of the job, they direct the interview towards 'checking you out'. This is a very different ball game from the more professional approach. While it may seem an easier proposition, questions can pose difficulties if they are badly thought out or poorly worded, appear to have little relevance to the job or fail to provide you with the opportunity to show your capabilities. Without good interview questions you may find you are unable to satisfy yourself that you could, or would want to, do the job. This sort of interview requires you to be on your toes and remain assertive in order to make sure the ground is covered to their satisfaction.

TACTICS FOR ANSWERING QUESTIONS

Aside from their factual content, the way answers are handled is also important. This is partly to do with communication skills (see Chapter 2) but also depends on other aspects of handling questions. Consider the following points.

ASK

It is impossible to give a good answer if the meaning of a question is not clear. Remember that some interviewers are not very good at articulating what they mean. If a question is not clear to you, do ask them to repeat it. They will most likely reword what they said and enlarge upon it. If you are still not totally sure you understand, say so or check your understanding of the question ('Do you mean what would I do if I suspected the customer was wrong?').

Some questions need qualifiers to establish clear parameters for your answer ('So you mean what would I do if the office were closed and all other designers had left?'). It is best to clarify points like this, otherwise what might be a good answer based on your understanding and interpretation of a question may seem way off beam to the interviewer, who was actually referring to something else.

FULL ANSWERS

A complaint made by one employer I spoke to concerned the failure of some candidates to open up and give full answers. Even allowing for nerves, some people seem to take the view that the less said, the sooner the whole thing will be over. This is not a good tactic. It may bring the interview to a quicker conclusion, but it won't reflect well on you. As Sue Bland at the Co-operative Bank pointed out, 'Interviewers like to see someone who can demonstrate they are interested and that they want to participate in the interview. It can be hard work when an interviewer has tried to relax someone, to get them talking so that they use up 80 per cent of the interview time talking, and then when they are asked open-ended questions [see below] they just close them down. It almost indicates a lack of interest in the job. And if two-thirds of the way through the interview a candidate is still being monosyllabic and not really responding openly to questions, that can be a problem.' Not giving full answers means selling yourself short.

KEEP IT SIMPLE AND DIRECT

If you keep replies simple and direct, it is easier for interviewers to see the point you are making. Don't waffle. You may be the fourth person interviewed that morning and they haven't yet had time for a coffee break. They may be flagging, their attention drifting. By giving information about yourself clearly and simply you will help to ensure they get the facts straight and do not overlook important points.

RIGHT AND WRONG ANSWERS

There are no right and wrong answers to many interview questions – although there are replies which may prove a better match to the employer's selection criteria than others. Bear this in mind when you listen to a question. Assess what they are really trying to establish and frame your reply not by guessing what will be seen as a right answer but by drawing on what your own knowledge, experience, attitudes and skills suggest. Interviewers don't operate on a tick/cross, marks-out-of-ten system in face-to-face interviews. Instead, through asking relevant questions, they aim to find out what you can bring to the job. For that there cannot possibly be a right or wrong set of answers, although some candidates will appear more suitable than others. What you can do is to give enough relevant and useful information about yourself to help them decide.

WATCH FOR SIGNALS

Just as interviewers will be watching for body language and presentation, so can you. Look out for helpful signals and make use of them. If the interview panel looks bored, give shorter, better-focused answers (see below). If it brightens up when you mention something in particular, make a mental note to emphasise it later or bring in a related piece of information. If it looks intensely at you, the members are probably touching on a subject important to them, so give a particularly thoughtful response. By watching interviewers carefully, you can pick up useful pointers about how to tackle, modify or direct your answers.

FACTS

'Keep replies fact-based. We don't want to hear the hype,' advised one top employer. By giving straight, hard facts to support answers you make an interviewer's task easier by providing sound material on which to base a decision. Otherwise his or her conclusions will rest on speculation about your abilities and experience – which may not provide an accurate picture.

KEEP IT RELEVANT

Bear in mind your mental dossier of information about the company and the job. Direct your answers on the relevance of your skills, qualifications and experience to those two things. A candidate may know all there is to know about budget-deficit controls because these formed a core part of the course he studied. A bare-bones answer – 'Yes, I understand all about them' – needs to be fleshed out with 'because I studied the various control systems in my degree course as well as writing my final thesis on the subject. When I worked at Jones & Co. during the summer vacation in 1996 I shadowed the Finance Director, who was working on developing new control systems for the company.' Nuggets of information like this may not have been highlighted in your application form, and although *you* know these are among the reasons why you think you could do the job, you have to share this knowledge openly with interviewers. They don't know what you know about yourself – unless you tell them. Spell it out. Promote yourself. Tell them about your achievements and experiences. They will want to hear about them.

POSITIVE/NEGATIVE

'Accentuate the positive; eliminate the negative' goes the song. There is more about how to deal with questions which touch on particularly sensitive or negative areas in the following chapter, but for the most part your replies should be painting you in the best possible light – without over-elaborating. Simply stake a rightful claim to your accomplishments, the contributions you have made in the past and all other relevant points which highlight your suitability for the job.

TYPES OF QUESTION

It is useful to understand the types of question an interviewer may use. Recognising them enables us to identify where the interviewer is coming from and how best to formulate a reply.

When practising for the interview, try to make sure sample questions are not all of the same type; they won't be in the real interview. It might be worth listening to questions asked during interviews on the TV or radio and seeing if you can identify the different kinds.

CLOSED QUESTIONS

'You worked at Jones & Co. until February last year?' 'Which team member took the project forward?' Closed questions are used mainly to establish facts and are often asked at the beginning of an interview to get the ball rolling. They lead to 'Yes' or 'No' or to some other simple reply.

Although these brief replies are normally sufficient, you need to be alert to occasions when a fuller answer would be better, especially if you feel too many closed questions are being asked and you are not getting the chance to demonstrate your suitability for the post well enough. Inexperienced and untrained interviewers are prone to do this. Watch out for it – and for occasions when a fuller answer may not be expected or required but would help serve your purpose and give a boost to your profile at an appropriate time.

OPEN QUESTIONS

'How was the situation resolved?' 'What was your contribution to improving the department?' Unlike closed questions, these make it almost impossible to give a simple 'Yes' or 'No' in reply. These are the more searching questions, the ones to which the interviewer expects a full answer and hopes that you will generally open up. These are the questions which provide you with the opportunity to talk with enthusiasm about how you helped resolve that problematic situation.

HYPOTHETICAL QUESTIONS

'What would you do if a client indicated he was unhappy with the service?' 'Imagine for a moment that four key members of staff were absent on the same day. How would you organise things?' Hypothetical questions present a set of circumstances or difficulties which might be encountered in the job, with the aim of trying to assess how effectively the applicant would cope. The answer may reveal to interviewers things like whether applicants are able to bring relevant experience to bear, what priorities, attitudes and levels of awareness they may or may not have, their ability to think on their feet, their problem-solving ability and the clarity of their thinking. If you are prepared, such questions can provide a useful indication of the sorts of situations which might be encountered in the job. To the unprepared candidate they simply bring shock.

If a hypothetical question relates to a familiar situation, you should have no difficulty in giving a full and reasoned answer. If it portrays an unusual situation or one which is outside your previous range of experience, then a little more care needs to be taken, particularly if the job being applied for is a promotion which will bring new responsibilities or form a stepping-stone to a new career. Direct experience may not be available to draw upon.

Try tackling the question by qualifying your answer: 'First I'd check the terms of the contract. Bearing those in mind, what I'd probably do is … '; 'How I'd deal with it would depend on whether we were in a peak production period, which members of staff were available as well as the budget for hiring temporary staff, but what I'd probably do is … '. If you are not sure what you would do in the situation described, say something which covers your back: show that you are aware of the constraints of the workplace; use your present level of experience and any relevant knowledge about the job and company. If your reply is unexpected, an interviewer may check on it or signal an opportunity to modify your answer by questioning the likely result of your course of action. Stay calm and simply follow through, taking into account specific issues they may have raised.

PROBING QUESTIONS

'You say you would investigate other options. How would you go about doing that?' 'What exactly did you mean when you referred to your past experience?' Probing questions aim to get beneath the surface of answers in order to clarify points. They aim to puncture waffle and, more constructively, to provide an opportunity for a more detailed reply to a subject already referred to in brief. Trained interviewers know the value of using probing questions; apart from making sure an answer isn't just hype, a probing question can also focus your answers and help you disclose information which you may be overlooking, perhaps because of interview nerves.

WHAT WILL THEY ASK?

Interviewers with professional training know that the best way to identify suitable candidates is to gear questions towards the key competences needed to do the job. This means that if the company has issued a job specification, your task in working out what they will ask you about is that much easier. For example, if one stated area of responsibility is 'To monitor the performance of freelance staff', then an interview question will try to establish whether you have the necessary experience and skills to carry out this function. One such question might be 'How would you go about monitoring the work of freelance staff?' or 'What experience do you have of supervising the work of contract staff?' Before the interview work through the job description and/or person specification, thinking of questions related to each point and remembering to formulate different types of question, not just the closed or open kind. Use whatever information you have about the job and the company to help construct answers, combining it with your own experience.

Apart from questions based directly on your application form or the job description, there may be other more general questions.

ICE-BREAKER

'Tell me a little about yourself'
If you go into an interview cold, without being prepared for this innocent-sounding question, it can throw you completely.

Where do you start? 'I was born in 1962 in Market Harborough'? And where do you end? At the point where you realise the interviewer has dozed off?

As the question is potentially so all-encompassing, check with the interviewer whether he wants to hear about the sort of person you are (that is, about your personal qualities) or about your career. By asking you immediately create a sense of rapport and extend the discussion. This shows you're not afraid of opening your mouth.

If he wants to know about your personal qualities, talk about those which relate to the workplace, such as being good with people, enjoying handling responsibility, being career-minded, etc. Include anything which you feel reflects the company's ethos or which relates to items in the job description. Give examples, where possible, to substantiate your claims.

If he wants to know about your career, *briefly* outline your present position as it relates to the job you are applying for (for example, 'During this time I've had the opportunity to develop team-building skills, which I understand would be key to this position'); why you have chosen this particular career path ('I've always been interested in new technology and also want a career which offers a real challenge'); what your broad aims are ('One day I would like to head up my own research team').

This is your opportunity to shine, to draw a thumbnail sketch of yourself in the best possible light. Remember the primacy–recency effect – shine at the start and you'll set the stage for the rest of the interview.

Remember to give full answers. Keep them relevant; keep them simple; keep them as brief as needs be. This may sound almost impossible to do – which is why practice helps.

QUESTIONS TO FIND OUT IF YOU CAN DO THE JOB

'What qualifications do you have for the job?'

When interviewers ask this question they are not referring just to academic qualifications. From what you know about the vacancy, highlight your particular experience, skills, personal qualities and academic qualifications. Mention only those which are relevant.

If this is your first job or if you are returning to work after a break (including unemployment), Bernard Kunerth at Coca-Cola suggests highlighting non-work, real-life examples which illustrate your relevant skills or experiences:

◆ Apart from my academic qualifications, I've had two work placements doing this sort of work and have a sound understanding of what's involved. I'm good at planning and organising things (every year at college I used to organise a fun-run for charity), and I get on well with people of all sorts, which is important when working with members of the public. I'm also familiar with the computer system you use here – it formed an integral part of the course I took.

Key points Although the candidate is applying for her first job, she manages to highlight relevant experience which may not be evident from the CV. The answer relates to the requirements of the job, which in this case involves planning customer-focused initiatives. Being familiar with a particular computer system won't in itself win the candidate the job but is a big plus and could be the thing which swings the job her way. An ineffective answer would only reiterate what was already on the CV or application form concerning academic qualifications.

'What experience do you feel you can bring to the job?'

Depending on the job, this may simply require an approach similar to the previous question's. For some vacancies it may help to mention life experiences:

◆ I've previously worked in the business sector, so I have sound commercial experience for ensuring effective use of funds, including controlling budgets, project management (which, of course, involves good people-management) and accountability. I also understand that the job involves developing a product line and marketing it to retail outlets. I successfully launched two new lines in my previous job and achieved the target of getting the product into 90 per cent of outlets in the giftware sector in the north-west.

◆ I've recently completed a counselling course on substance abuse and have spent the last year working as a volunteer with Al Anon. The work involved counselling people over the phone as well as in person. A close friend developed a drink problem five years ago, so I can bring to the job not just professional training but also my own personal experience.

Key points Both applicants are applying for a post which they haven't held before; however, they manage to bring to the fore key points from their past experience which are of direct relevance to the one they are applying for. A poor answer would concentrate on job titles and places of work, overlooking work on special projects and valuable personal or unpaid work experiences relevant to the vacancy.

'Describe the main areas of responsibility in your present job'

These should be relatively easy to describe if you're prepared; if not, you could end up either going into too much detail or, conversely, missing important points. Again pick out responsibilities which relate to the job you're applying for.

◆ I oversee the production of three of the company's five publications, one of them the in-house magazine. I liaise with editors, freelance designers and printers as well as the distribution companies. I'm responsible not only for putting the magazines together but also for getting the best price for the job. This is an important part of the work because we operate within very tight budgets, especially on the in-house magazine. I understand this type of publication is the mainstay of your work.

Key points Not all jobs involve the same level of responsibility or involvement, so this candidate has wisely chosen to highlight budgetary responsibilities and her experience of working on the sorts of publications in which the company to which she is applying specialises. Mentioning the types of people with whom she has had to liaise shows she is used to dealing with a wide range of professionals rather than working to a single line manager. Her failure to describe the full range of her relevant responsibilities would sell herself short.

'What can you offer the company?'/ 'Why do you want to work for us?'

First you have to know what the company wants; for this you need to have done the necessary research. Then, in answer to the question, let them know you understand what their aims, reputation, achievements and needs are and highlight how your experience and personal qualities fit. They want to hear about the benefits you can offer, so go ahead and tell them about your relevant previous achievements.

♦ I have a sharp mind, love new challenges, enjoy working in a team – and I've got the experience. Last year I helped to successfully introduce the just-in-time principle, which has already saved the company nearly £250,000. I fully appreciate that controlling overheads is key in your sector at the moment, especially with the new competition from South America, and I understand you want someone to spearhead the introduction of this way of working here.

♦ You're the best PR company working for small businesses in the south-east. The campaigns you ran for Bert's Co. and Swank & Frank were fantastic. Over the last few years I've worked very successfully with a number of small businesses – almost exclusively during the past year. This is where my strength lies. I have the experience and am keen to work for a young, go-ahead company like yours where I can make a direct contribution to helping your clients succeed.

Key points　The first candidate knows that the job involves teamwork, and his research has flagged the fierce competition from abroad. He makes use of this vital information and ties his answer in with what he has gleaned from the job description. The second answer also reveals that the candidate has done her homework and understands the business. She builds a bridge between what the company needs and what she is able to offer. What wouldn't work in either case is a reply that is pure hype – one that is not job/company-focused and does not substantiate claims with fact.

'Why should I offer you the job?'

The bluntness of the question can be disorientating. In fact, it is a straightforward opening. What the interviewer really wants from this question is for you to point out your qualifications for the job and what you can bring to it. To answer the question well you need to study the requirements of the job and how you fulfil them. There's no harm in making the answer as direct as the question.

- I've consistently exceeded sales targets over the last year, successfully broken into the academic market and expanded my sales team by 50 per cent. I'm an achiever, know the competition inside out and am ready for the sort of challenge the job offers.

- You want someone who has experience of working with your client group, who can handle the work you've outlined and who understands the constraints of the job. I have five years' experience and am familiar with all aspects of the work. In addition, I can bring valuable experience of both living and working in Europe, along with fluency in French and German. It's a new market you want to break into, and I have the relevant experience and skills.

Key points It is clear from both responses that the candidates not only understand the requirements of the job and the company but are confident in their abilities to fulfil them. They tell it like it is, but they manage to convey to the interviewer some very sound reasons for their being employed. What you don't want to convey, at any cost, is how desperate you are for the job and how it will be the answer to your dreams. The reason you should be offered the job is not because it will solve your problems but because you can help to solve the company's.

'What have you achieved in your present job?'

Don't be tempted to mention everything from clearing your desk to managing to stick it out so long with an awful boss – an achievement in itself. What the questioner really wants to know about are achievements which are of direct relevance to the vacancy the company is trying to fill. Prepare carefully for this one; know which key points will make the most impact. Don't waffle and confuse the interviewer with unimportant details.

◆ Since I started at Jones & Co. two years ago I've gained an in-depth knowledge of the ZX570 stock-accounting system and have successfully trained four other users. In addition I suggested to management setting up a Web page, which they agreed to try. I completed the project earlier on this year, and so far it's been a huge success with 50 per cent more visitors to the site than expected.

Key points Knowledge of this particular stock-accounting system is vital since it is the one which the new company is about to introduce. They have a number of staff who will need training in how to use it, so the fact that the interviewee has trained other users is important to mention. Although the new company has said nothing about wanting to launch a Web page, the mention of it demonstrates forward-thinking, commercial awareness and a wide range of skills.

'What are you good at?'

Again highlight only those accomplishments which are of direct relevance to the job. These could include a broad range of skills, including interpersonal skills, leadership, being good at motivating others. Avoid focusing on the more obvious aspects of your work – every other candidate will be doing that. False modesty won't help here. Simply state, as a matter of fact, your particular strengths.

◆ Apart from design work, I'm good at taking briefs from clients, getting them to flesh out their ideas and establishing what they want from me as a designer. I'm good at presenting concepts and communicating my ideas to clients – and I always work to deadline.

Key points The candidate could have talked about specific aspects of design work and her skills with a drawing pen, but bringing skills with clients to the fore is more important – employers can judge the artwork for themselves. Working to deadline is key to keeping customers satisfied. It also shows good organisation of work and time. It won't help your cause if you say, 'Well, I'm good at computer graphics.' So will half the other candidates.

'What do you find most difficult?'

You don't want to draw attention to your shortcomings or turn this part of the interview into a confessional, so be prepared. Mention something from the past that wouldn't apply to the new job, or try to turn the question around.

◆ I hate working in Maidstone and would love to be back in London again.

◆ The end of the financial year always creates an extra workload, but I organise it so that I start drawing up the accounts six weeks before the end of the year. This means that when the year-end comes I have only a small amount of extra work to put in, and it also means I don't fall behind with the rest of my work.

Key points The first reply mentioned a 'safe' topic – something which was related only tangentially to the new job. The second answer shows how a problematic area has been positively dealt with. This reply avoids admitting to having any weaknesses and has turned the question around to demonstrate good problem-solving and time-management skills. Steer clear of baring your soul and saying how awful you find the accounting year-end and how it throws you every time it comes round.

QUESTIONS TO FIND OUT IF YOU WANT TO DO THE JOB

'Tell me what you know about our company'

This question invites you demonstrate your interest in the job and company. The question is asking about motivation. If a candidate gives an answer which clearly shows he has not bothered to find out anything about the operation, it will be interpreted as a lack of enthusiasm. As you mention main points about the company, including items like its mission statement and any recent major developments, tie in any of your own specific abilities or experiences which you feel might complement the company's aims and help contribute to the company's success. A model answer will establish the idea of a relationship between the employer and employee in the interviewer's mind.

◆ I know the company is a relative newcomer to the market but has already made significant gains over the competition. Introducing a line which targets the older end of the market seems to have paid off. The company I work for at present is only just waking up to the potential there, but I've been involved in drawing up a new marketing plan to target this group. Your company has also hit the headlines with its strong slogan, which promises, and by all accounts delivers, a higher quality of service than any of your rivals.

Key points The answer demonstrates a good level of awareness about the company, its products and its current position in the market. Although the question required an answer about the company, the candidate has managed to use the opportunity to divulge additional useful information about himself and to highlight further the relevance of his experience to the job.

'Why do you want the job?'

Again, the interviewer wants to find out about your motivation, not about what you think the company can do for you. Where do your enthusiasms for the work lie? Talk about the challenges you see the job providing, as well as the opportunities for being able to make a positive contribution.

♦ I've successfully worked as deputy editor for the past five years on leisure magazines, but my background is in computers and IT, so this post is ideal. Not only do I have the skills and experience to take on a full editorship at this point in my career, but I have the drive and ambition to make this title succeed. I see where the competition is stealing the edge at the moment and feel confident I can do for this magazine what I managed to achieve with *Relax* magazine and *MX*.

Key points   The answer gets right down to it. She wants the job because she wants the challenge and is confident in her ability to turn the magazine round and make it work. She backs up her beliefs and puts them in context with reference to her past achievements, which may not be evident from her CV alone. She's obviously done her homework on the title too. It would be a much less effective answer if she had simply focused on her own ambitions.

'How do you see yourself five years from now?'
Companies like to see evidence of potential – and they like to see highly motivated candidates. Having said this, judge how best to answer this question based on what you know of the job and the company. Do they want a high-flyer who wants to zoom through the ranks, or are they looking for a steady worker who will be happy to stay in the same post until retirement? Whichever applies, it's probably fair to say that evidence of company loyalty goes down well with most employers. Without preparing for this sort of question it would be easy to give an answer which puts you out of the running – or at least makes them wary about the degree of fit between you and them.

♦ I see myself working in the same field, but I would hope to have developed sufficiently to take on a wider range of responsibilities and be more directly involved in implementing new initiatives. The company's plans to develop the former Eastern-bloc market particularly interest me, and I could have quite a bit to contribute on that front. I've been monitoring developments over there for the past couple of years. I think it has lots of potential.

♦ I'm looking for a steady job, but I'm happy to learn new things as need be. I understand the present system might be computerised in the future. Well, I'm used to word-processing and I'd be really interested to learn about spreadsheets and databases and how to use them.

Key points Although the candidates are applying for very different positions, both replies manage to convey that the applicants are professional in their respective fields and have a good awareness of the company's plans. They have managed to turn the focus of the question around to what they can do for the company, so that their replies don't become a litany of personal ambitions. They would have done less well if they had given replies which focused entirely on what they wanted to achieve without regard for how their achievements would benefit the company.

'What do you enjoy most about the work you do?'
This is relatively straightforward to answer, but do keep the reply focused on what you know they are looking for and what the job demands. It will only demonstrate an acute mismatch if they have to listen to you enthusing about computers when there would be no involvement with them in the new job. The question invites a brief, selective answer – what is enjoyed 'most' – so don't allow the answer to ramble.

♦ I really enjoy having contact with customers, which I understand is what this job would mainly involve.

♦ I particularly enjoy working as part of a team, although at Perkins we don't work like that all the time, just on special projects. This is what strongly appeals to me about this job – having my own area of responsibility but working with a more team-centred approach.

Key points Both replies home in on key features of the new job. This has the effect of reassuring the interviewer that the candidates are cut out for the type of work, or way of working, which would be expected of them. Actual skills are less important. It wouldn't have furthered their cause much if their replies had concentrated on the more mundane, routine aspects of their current jobs.

'What do you enjoy least?'

Be cautious about answering any question which could expose weaknesses or provide reasons not to employ you. Instead try to present your answer in such a way that it becomes positive in the eyes of the new employer.

♦ There's little I don't actually enjoy, but what I am looking for is the chance to use my languages more, which is why this particular job appeals. Not only do I speak Chinese but I spent two years working in China. I understand you've just won a new contract to build a factory in Beijing.

♦ I'd like to do more Web page design. It's only part of the work I do at present in a small company. I designed the pages for the Citizen's Society, which has led to a trebling of their membership. I understand that Web page design would be an important part of this job.

Key points Both candidates have managed to avoid admitting to anything they don't like about their current jobs and have focused instead on an aspect of the new job which appeals to them. Again, both have used the opportunity to remind the interviewer of specific credentials and reinforced the impression of their suitability for the job. What would not have gone down well is if they had concentrated on some hated aspect of their present work – it would have done nothing to help sell themselves to the interviewer. Every question should be seen as an opportunity to provide another reason why they *should* employ you, not why they shouldn't.

'Why did you leave your last job?'

Be up-front – but tactful. If you resigned, think about what was lacking in the job which you see this one providing. For example, if your last position was a dead-end job, you could answer that you are looking for a company in which there are opportunities for promotion. (If you were sacked, see the next chapter.)

- ◆ I didn't feel I was being stretched enough. I'd been doing the same work for some time and was ready to take on more responsibilities, but the opportunities weren't coming up. So I'd be very keen to work for this company where, because of its size, I'd be able to make a much fuller contribution.

- ◆ As you know, Roberts & Sons is a very traditional company with a solid, stable list of clients. Although I've enjoyed my time there, I realise I've also got a lot to offer in a more dynamic and competitive environment – like The Vision.

Key points Without running down their previous employer or falling into the trap of admitting to past failings, each candidate has managed to turn a negative into a positive for the new employer. They've sold them the idea that their company would benefit from currently unexploited talents. Conversely, criticising their past employer or complaining about how dull the work was would provide no reason at all why the new employer should hire them.

'This job involves a much higher level of responsibility than your current one. How do you feel about that?'

The interviewer wants to make sure you're going after the job because you're ready to take the next step up in your career and not because you're attracted to the salary increase or added perks. He wants reassurance. Your answer should provide it:

- ◆ I've been an assistant warden for three years now, and in that time I've successfully covered in the warden's absence and been in sole charge on many occasions, once for a period of three months. Over the last year I've stood in for him at meetings with the board and at case conferences. I've also taken a number of in-service training courses in preparation for this next step in my career. I'm not only ready for greater responsibilities, I'm looking forward to them.

Key points   The candidate reassures the interviewer by highlighting his ability to take on more responsibility. Covering for a superior would not necessarily appear on the CV, so this is a good opportunity to let him know about it, backing up the information with reference to additional training. The answer is rounded off by reassurance of the interviewee's enthusiasm for her job – not the perks that go with it. A poor answer would have been defensive ('I'm as good as the next person'), or would have failed to convey both experience and confidence in the interviewee's own abilities.

'As senior project manager, what would you see as your main aims?'
The interviewer knows what the job entails, so isn't interested in hearing you recite the job description. The answer to a question about aims is to get you to focus on the broader picture and where you see not just yourself but in this case the whole department and the staff under your direction.

◆   Apart from ensuring the smooth running of the department and the projects it handles, I'd be aiming to turn an already skilled team of project managers into the best there is. I see professional development as being central to this. I'm talking not about straight project-management skills but about a wider range of issues, such as team-building, conflict-resolution and negotiating skills. Clients may not see these in operation, but they'll feel the benefit when projects are completed on time and within budget, and it's that which builds a company's reputation in this field.

Key points   The candidate is showing that he is ambitious for the department under his direction and not only for himself. He clearly indicates he's not just a firefighter or front person but someone who wants his whole staff to excel. He neatly ties this in with reference to the benefits of his approach to both the client group and the company. This candidate's motivation is clearly in the right place.

QUESTIONS TO FIND OUT IF YOU WILL FIT

'How do you feel about taking instructions from someone?'

How you relate to authority is especially a concern if you are a younger applicant or someone wanting to down-shift from a more senior position. It helps to reassure the interviewer that this poses no difficulties and, if you can, illustrate your reply with an example of a situation in which you acted under instruction and learned something constructive from the experience.

- So long as I'm told clearly what I have to do or what's expected of me it's fine, and I've learned now to ask if I haven't had something explained to me properly or I don't understand, especially while I've been helping out as a volunteer at the Five Ways Centre.

- Although I've been used to issuing instructions to others, I was only ever part of the chain of command – someone further up used to tell me what to do. Unless you own the company, you're always going to be following someone's instructions, and even then the customers dictate what you do more often than not. I'm very comfortable with taking instructions. I'll relish being able to concentrate on the work in hand.

Key points   Both candidates have managed to give ample reassurance that their experience has equipped them to work under direction. Mentioning voluntary work is a good ploy. The more senior worker makes the point that we all have to take direction to a greater or lesser degree and lets the inter-viewer know that his new-found focus is not management but doing the job itself instead.

'Give an example of how you resolved a difficulty with another member of staff.'
Avoid drawing attention to major problems you may have had with someone; try to talk instead about a situation which demonstrates your negotiating, leadership or other skills with people. Accentuate the positive.

- I haven't had any real difficulties. I find that if things aren't running as smoothly as they should, it's best to talk it through straight away with the other person, whether it's a colleague, a line manager or a client. The problem is often lack of communication or a simple misunderstanding.

- I had two team members who couldn't seem to get on together. I didn't want this to affect their work, so I spoke to each separately, in private, about the problem. After hearing both sides I mediated between the two and helped them reach an amicable agreement. They couldn't communicate with each other, but having a third person to speak on their behalf seemed to solve things.

Key points The first candidate chose to give a broad-based answer, indicating that she is relaxed and confident in her interpersonal relationships, although an interviewer may press for an actual example. The second candidate gives one but avoids a 'He said ... She said ... ', blow-by-blow account of the upset and instead demonstrates good mediation skills.

'Give an example of a time when you worked as a member of a team.'
If team-working is an important aspect of the new job, they will be keen to see evidence of your ability to work well with others – not everyone can. If you have not had the opportunity

to work as a team member in your professional life, use non-work experience to demonstrate this ability.

◆ Although I haven't worked as a team member in my present job, I'm an active member of a charity fundraising team. We have regular meetings and work together on getting our fundraising projects off the ground. I really enjoy working in this way, when everyone just gets on with it and pulls together. You can achieve a lot more that way.

Key points   Although the candidate hasn't had experience of working in a team in his job, he brings in his experience outside work. Not only that, but he expresses his enjoyment of working in this way and understands the importance of pulling together.

'How do you see yourself fitting in here?'

To answer this well, and not respond with empty enthusiasm, you really do need to have done your homework on the company. It requires you to show an understanding of the company culture and how your own personal qualities, drives and ambitions fit in with theirs. Without evidence of a good fit there will be doubt in the employer's mind about whether you would be a successful member of staff.

◆ I've worked in this sector for most of my working life. I understand the culture and like your way of working. It would suit me because here you seem willing to take the sorts of calculated risk which others won't. With my experience and background I feel I'm more than up to the challenge of fronting this new operation.

◆ I see myself fitting in very well. I like the company's focus on quality of care rather than on cutting costs. I believe this is the way forward – looking at long-term success rather than short-term gain. I also like the more team-centred approach. I'm used to this way of working and find it creates a much more productive work environment.

Key points Both candidates sum up key points about the companies, how they operate and how they feel they would fit in. The degree of organisational fit won't be decided by interviewers on the strength of this question alone, but it provides the opportunity for them to learn how candidates see themselves in relation to the company.

STRESS INTERVIEWS

All interviews are stressful, but some are expressly designed to tax candidates under pressure. The approach is properly employed only when it relates to the job – especially management positions. Two-thirds of companies use this technique at times when recruiting graduates.

Tactics may include:

◆ interrupting

◆ acting aggressively

◆ different interviewers firing questions in quick succession

◆ asking personal questions

◆ changing the planned course of the interview

◆ contradicting

◆ acting in a condescending manner

◆ ridiculing replies.

All these are aimed at unnerving and unsettling you. Your best strategy is to remain calm and polite and not allow yourself to be drawn. Practice will obviously help.

'What do you think of the other candidates?'
With a question like this, the interviewer is testing how easily you might be led, how far you will go to please authority, how readily you fall prey to point-scoring. Beware.

◆ I didn't have time to talk to any of them.

◆ I really couldn't say, as I don't know them.

'But they look a bit wet behind the ears, don't you think?'
The interviewer may try to press you further. Stick to your guns.

◆ As I said, I didn't spend much time with them.

◆ As I said, I really couldn't say.

Key points The answers are direct and simple and demonstrate a firm but polite refusal to be drawn. They confirm that these candidates are above passing even light-hearted negative comments, which would mark them down. So would agreeing with the interviewer that the others look inexperienced.

'Don't you find your weight/height/etc. an embarrassment?'
How calm will you stay in a situation where remarks may get personal? How easily are you ruffled? Can you deal with cutting comments?

◆ No.

◆ On the contrary. People can't exactly ignore someone of my size, which I've found to be an advantage.

Key points 'No' can be said in any number of ways. Here it needs to be said calmly, without a hint of offence or defensiveness. The second reply is rather more tongue-in-cheek. Decide for yourself whether it would be appropriate. But avoid a humorous reply – it could be seen as a defensive ploy. Showing irritation would obviously count against you.

'Don't you find it difficult to cope on your present salary?'
People can be very touchy about their personal finances, especially when the question seems to cast a slight on their earning capacity. Don't be defensive. This is another question to test how easily you get unnerved.

◆ I budget well and live comfortably within my means.

Key points Including a reference to budgeting goes down well with any employer. They like to know their employees aren't likely to run into financial problems. Needless to say, it's especially important if the job you're being interviewed for involves financial management.

'Who do you hope will win the next election?'
Unless the job you're applying for has direct links with a political party or would obviously benefit from the election of one or another, it's best to keep the answer as neutral as possible. What they're on the look-out for is any extreme views. If you're unprepared for this it's hard to form a succinct answer.

◆ Well, it looks a pretty even match between the two main parties, so it's anybody's guess, really.

Key points This manages to side-step the issue. A more definite answer would run the risk of opening up a political debate, which you don't want. You might find yourself unknowingly arguing with the chair of a local party – one you wouldn't vote for.

'How do you feel about having a black/female/Moslem/etc. boss?'
The Sex Discrimination Act 1975 and Race Relations Act 1976 make it illegal to discriminate against anyone on grounds of their sex, race, creed or nationality. An interviewer may want to assess whether candidates have any discriminatory tendencies themselves.

◆ It's of no consequence what colour/sex/creed/etc. some-one is. The only thing that matter to me is that we all pull together as a team and get the results we're after.

Key points Surprisingly, some people do give away hidden biases: a slight intake of breath, eyes wide open, raised eye-brows, a longer pause than normal before answering. This candidate, however, shows clearly that his focus is on the job and has even used the opportunity to reinforce the fact that he is a team player who likes to get results.

'I'm not sure if you're up to the job.'
A trick statement to see whether you'll rise to the challenge and convince them otherwise.

◆ What particular reservations do you have?

◆ I may not have that many years' experience, but I don't think that's a problem. My track record, academically and in my present job, shows I have ability. I'm confident of my skills, I'm keen and I'm ready for this sort of challenge.

Key points Launching into a defensive answer may not be your best bet. By throwing the ball back into their court, as the first response does, you can find out their specific doubts and form your answer accordingly. The second candidate meets the interviewer's objection and answers assertively showing enthusiasm and confidence. This is what the interviewer wants to hear.

In a stress interview be prepared for each of your replies to be probed further ('But surely being your weight/height *must* cause problems for you'). Some interviewers won't let you off the hook easily. They're hoping to make you uncomfortable and embarrassed. Stick with your answers, stay calm and remember what their intention is. On occasion it can be a useful ploy to turn the questioning around, so long as you can do so without sounding aggressive ('I can assure you that my size isn't a problem for me, but does my weight bother you?'). This can often break the questioning down.

BLUNDERS

Verbal blunders – we all make them. As soon as the words are out we know that we've said the wrong thing or that our words have been taken in the wrong way.

If this happens at interview, you may be lucky and have a good interviewer who checks on your reply and delves deeper, perhaps realising the inappropriateness of the response. Otherwise admit the blunder openly and establish that you'd like a second chance to deal with the question. Say something like:

- ◆ I don't think that was really the response you were looking for, was it? Could you repeat the question, as I think I may have misunderstood it?

- ◆ I don't think I expressed myself very well there. What I was trying to say was ...

Admissions of guilt are much better than verbose attempts to waffle on and cover up the mistake. All that happens then is that you inevitably talk yourself into a corner. By openly admitting a mistake you demonstrate an ability to handle yourself well in an awkward situation, demonstrating social competence, good communications skills (even though a blunder has been made) and alertness. So all is definitely not lost.

The more professional and experienced the interviewer, the more easily the interview will progress. But, whatever interview situation you find yourself in, your ability to handle the questions and the quality of your replies will depend on how well you can demonstrate the relevance of your experience to the job and aims of the company by backing up your answers with facts, examples and feeling. To employers motivation and enthusiasm for the job are as important as the right qualifications, and they will be the determining factors at interview.

Handling Sensitive Topics

In an ideal world interviewers know what they are about, conduct streamlined interviews and help candidates give of their best. As we all know, in reality the world of interviews, like everything else, is far from ideal.

In particular, there are questions you dread – about gaps in employment, time spent in prison, the fact that you were sacked from two previous jobs – questions touching on extremely sensitive areas.

A natural reaction is to pretend to ourselves that these weaknesses don't exist, and to try not to think about them at all. Yet anything which employers identify from your application form as a potential problem is bound to be put under the spotlight. The only realistic thing you can do, therefore, is prepare yourself beforehand and have your answers ready. Preparation will help you avoid subconsciously sending out distress signals through the quality of your answers and body language.

Here are some give-aways:

◆ a hand which starts to hover around the mouth – it suggests that you are trying to cover up what you say

◆ answering the question in a slower or quieter voice, or a faster or louder one, than you had been using up to that point; try to keep your tone even

◆ a sudden change of position – it signals that the question has, literally, made you feel uncomfortable

- sudden displacement activities, like fidgeting, coughing or clearing the throat

- a sudden change of expression or a frozen smile, blushing, clenched jaws and breaking eye contact. Remaining impassive will signal you are not troubled.

How a response is made can also be a give-away. Researchers have shown that acting defensively is not a good tactic. Making up an excuse or trying to justify oneself can have an adverse effect on an interviewer's judgement of a candidate. Using ill-health, drink problems or mental illness to explain away a poor employment record also fails to enhance a candidate's chances of a job offer. A 'poor me' attitude can work with some employers, who respond by deciding to be big-hearted and give the applicant a break. However, this is a gamble which may backfire, especially with more professional interviewers. More forthright and confident approaches are likely to be more successful. Being prepared and dealing openly and honestly with awkward questions are much better options and can register positively with interviewers.

EMPLOYMENT DIFFICULTIES

A sensitive subject for many of us may be previous (or current) jobs. As interviewers will have a full work record in front of them, it is hard to imagine they will overlook this. It's essential to be prepared.

QUICK SUCCESSION OF JOBS

'Your work record shows you haven't held down a job for more than six months. Why is that?'
If you are in the early stages of working life, this question is less of a problem. It can often take a few false starts to find something that really suits you. Try to convey the impression that the array of jobs reflects a conscious decision on your part to explore different avenues. Mention what it is you are looking for – which other positions have failed to provide and which this one will: a more appropriate level of challenge,

joining a highly motivated workforce, working for a go-ahead company. You can also mention how each job has helped you move towards your present goal:

◆ When I left school/college/university I wasn't clear about which field I wanted to work in. Now that I've had the chance to try out different ones I know that this is the area for me and this the type of forward-looking company I want to work for.

◆ In each case I'd been led to believe I'd have a much greater level of responsibility than I was actually given. It became obvious pretty soon that it wasn't going to happen. From what you've told me so far, this post seems more suited to my qualifications and experience, and it would provide the level of challenge I'm looking for.

Key points Both candidates' replies show that, far from being job-hoppers, they have made a concerted effort to find a job in which they could use best what they have to offer. In addition they test their understanding of what the present company and job could provide. If they are wrong, their replies should open up the discussion so that both parties reach a better understanding of whether the candidates would be suited to the post. The first may be asked more about why she thinks this area is the one for her. The second could find the interviewer asking about what previous jobs didn't provide and what his understanding is of the challenge of the advertised job. Answers which wouldn't do well here would focus on criticism of previous employers, excuses or inadequate replies that would indicate a certain lack of awareness of, or concern about, progress to date.

UNRELATED WORK EXPERIENCE

'Your previous experience is in a very different field. What makes you think you'd be suited to this post?'/'Why do you want to change?'

Perhaps you are being interviewed for a job in sales, but your previous experience has been in administration. Or your first two jobs were as a conference organiser, but now you are applying for a position in social care. Your answer will indicate whether you are making a reasoned decision, have the necessary commitment or are just jumping around for the sake of a change.

The first thing to remember is that if they have called you to interview, there is undoubtedly something about your application which interests them, otherwise they wouldn't have bothered to take your application this far. Also people generally have very sound reasons for wanting to change direction. It is nothing to be ashamed of, but without being prepared for the question it is easy to slip into giving a defensive response.

Think about what it is that appeals to you about the new job (other than things such as a higher salary or fringe benefits). Identify what it was about the previous job which failed to satisfy. Clarify the process you went through to bring you to the point of change. For example, the admin person may have had to sit in on a sales briefing and decided he liked what he saw. The conference organiser may have realised the pursuit of commercial profit was not satisfying. In your answer draw out relevant experience gained in other work environments which would transfer, such as organisational skills, interpersonal skills, leadership, etc. And, of course, make sure you mention any courses you have attended (or plan to attend) that relate to the new job.

◆ I've worked in administration for ten years now and have been in my present job with Sellemore's for just over a year. In this time I've had a lot of involvement with the sales teams and become really interested in their work, and I've started to learn quite a lot about their role. One thing I do know is that to be a good salesperson you have to believe in your product, and I've always been interested in office equipment – especially as I use so much of it in my job. And I know yours is the best. I think sales has always appealed to me, and now I know more about it I'm confident I could do it and that it's the job for me.

Key points The answer briefly outlines what brought him to the point of realising he wanted to change career – not the money, company car or bonus schemes but doing a job which he realises he is cut out for and has always been interested in. He lets the interviewer know about the relevance of his experience and why he wants to work for them – because their equipment is the best. He rounds off his answer with a positive statement about his confidence in his own abilities. The interviewer will probably use his reply to ask more probing questions which will give the candidate an opportunity to expand on his answer. It would be an ineffective reply if it concentrated on the negative aspects of the job which the candidate wanted to leave behind.

UNRELATED ACADEMIC QUALIFICATIONS

'Why are you applying for a job in banking when your degree is in earth sciences?'

Much the same goes for answering a question about disparities between qualifications and the job as one about unrelated work experience, so read through the previous entry. Employers are unsettled when they spot mismatches, as what they are looking for is a good, positive fit between an applicant and the job.

To prepare for this question be clear in your own mind why the job appeals and what contribution you feel you can make. Concentrate on the non-academic qualifications you have for the post: enthusiasm for the product or company, being good at team-working, having a flair for figures and so on. And make use of the fact that a non-linear progression demonstrates flexibility – something for which employers are now on the look-out.

♦ Although I enjoyed my degree I've since realised that, in terms of a career, working in the financial sector is what really appeals. It was the analysis, statistics and economic aspects of the subject I studied which always interested me most (I was treasurer of the student union), and meeting your representatives on the milk round, finding out about the opportunities here and what a go-ahead company you are really decided things for me. Your emphasis on developing a multi-skilled workforce and introducing the team-work approach particularly appeals.

Key points The answer shows how to highlight relevant points and tie them in with what is known about the job and the company. The candidate manages to slip in a detail about extra-curricular activities which may have escaped the interviewer's notice.

FAILURE TO THRIVE

'It seems you've been in your current post for some considerable time. You haven't been promoted?'
If you have been with the same company for a long time, doing the same thing, this may raise doubts in an employer's mind about whether you could prove to be dead wood, looking for another easy ride, or are not particularly good at your job (otherwise you would have been promoted). The reality could be little or no internal movement in the company since you joined and lack of opportunities for promotion. But this question is, in fact, an opportunity to demonstrate your commitment to a job and company, loyalty to customers or clients, the depth (if not breadth) of your experience and your motivation, enthusiasm and readiness for what the new job has to offer. If you have been preparing yourself for such a move by attending training courses or gaining relevant experience in a non-work environment, do mention this.

- ◆ It's a small company, but I've valued the in-depth experience I've been able to gain over the years – albeit at the expense of climbing the ladder by moving on. I know my job, I'm good at it and you can see I'm someone who's loyal and dedicated to an employer and their clients. But I am ready for a new challenge. Last year I attended a number of professional courses, most in my own time. I listed them on my application form.

◆ I've enjoyed developing in the job over the years, progressing with each new development, like those which followed the introduction of new legislation, and helping to implement reorganisations. Although I've stayed in the same post, there have been a number of changes. The company has been a good employer to work for, but now I'm keen to broaden my experience and build on the knowledge I've gained.

Key points   No defensiveness in these answers. The candidates relate the value of having stayed in post for a number of years and, far from standing still, they give the impression of having made continuous progress despite there being no promotion to indicate this. If you think an interviewer has overlooked something important, such as the first candidate's professional development, it's just as well to draw attention to it.

BEING SACKED

Dishonesty

Trying to cover up dishonesty won't work. Its better to demonstrate that you are mature enough to assume responsibility for your actions by explaining what it was that took place. If there are any, mention briefly any mitigating circumstances, such as peer pressure or severe financial hardship. Conclude with a sentence which shows that you realise whatever you did was wrong/stupid/out of character. Indicate in what way you have paid your dues. Keep it simple and direct.

◆ I was caught selling some stock on the side and was dismissed on the spot. They decided to prosecute. I suppose because everyone else was doing it I thought it was OK. Of course it was not, and I've no one to blame but myself. I've never done anything like that before. It was stupid of me. As a result, I was put on probation and now hope I can put it all behind me.

Key points   No cover-ups: just a straight, clean admission of guilt and what took place. Of course, an employer may still decide not to take the risk of employing you. That's up to them. But a fair-minded interviewer should find a reply like this acceptable.

Difference of opinion
This can be a truly tricky issue but, whatever you may feel about your last boss, don't ever be tempted to criticise him during the interview. Focus on the nub of the problem and how it affected your ability to do the job. There is normally a good root cause. Your task is to touch on the problem, explain how you attempted to resolve it, show that you are not bitter and close with a positive point. If there was a high turnover of staff at your last company, mention that too.

◆   I've the greatest respect for my former supervisor and felt I had a real contribution to make, but it became obvious that my opinion wasn't welcome. I did try to discuss it with him and even took advice from other senior colleagues. Eventually I decided to go out on a limb, which wasn't a wise move in hindsight, but I'm glad that this job involves a more integrated, team-work approach.

Key points   The candidate avoids the sour-grapes syndrome while explaining what the problem was. The final sentence links her reply with the present vacancy and not only brings out the positive side to the underlying difficulty with her previous boss but also helps to move the interview along.

Time-keeping
Poor time-keeping often reflects lack of interest in the job rather than innate laziness. Mention those things which failed to motivate you or even demotivated you (and which are not features of the new job). Highlight aspects of the new one which do appeal. If the job has similar characteristics and you see yourself running into much the same difficulties, perhaps

a rethink about whether you should be going after a different sort of job would be worthwhile.

- ◆ I realise that the real problem was that there wasn't enough to keep me interested, and when I asked about having my name put forward for further training they said no. That's why this job appeals. Although I'd be doing the same work some of the time, you said you train people here so that they can work on a rota system. That sounds great. Do you train people for higher levels too?

Key points This candidate may have been seen as a slacker in his previous job, but his reply shows clearly that the real problem was lack of motivation. He's obviously got a lot to offer an employer and is ambitious. It sounds as though he has potential, and the interviewer should take his application seriously. Had he not prepared his answer, he could have been caught out by an embarrassed admission that he didn't know why he had been so bad at time-keeping. A reply like that would be almost guaranteed to make the interviewer wary.

Poor performance

The same goes for poor performance. It could be that the previous job was very different from what you had imagined it would be; these things happen. Demonstrate to the interviewer the good match between you and the new job, and show you have done your research into what it entails. He will be worried about your ability to do the work, so you need to reassure him about your enthusiasm and competences.

- ◆ The work wasn't as demanding as it promised to be, and I just wasn't doing what I'd been trained for. It was mostly low-grade work. I understand this post requires someone with my qualifications and I'm keen to put my knowledge to full use. Does the job entail scheduling as well?

Key points Briefly and succinctly, the candidate has reassured the interviewer that the problem was lack of motivation and a mismatch between what the job had initially promised and the reality. She sounds eager to find her proper niche. Asking keenly about a likely aspect of the work helps to keep the interview moving along. An unprepared candidate trying to formulate a quick answer could end up sounding guilty and defensive.

Poor attendance

If the problem was caused by lack of interest and commitment to the job, see **Time-keeping** and **Poor performance** above. If it was caused by personal problems, such as chronic illness, alcohol abuse, family difficulties, drugs or mental-health problems, the employer will want reassurance about the measures taken to remedy the situation. They will need more than platitudes ('I've turned over a new leaf'). They will want concrete evidence that the situation has changed. References from professional support workers to back up your claims may help.

♦ My teenage son had a lot of problems, which did affect my work record over quite a long period. He's now sorted himself out. This note from his social worker should explain things.

♦ I developed a problem with alcohol which, as you can see from my application form, cost me my job. Since then I've had professional help and have also sorted out a few personal problems which were at the root of it all. Here's a report from the counsellor I've been seeing and one from my GP to confirm I'm back on course.

Key points　Both candidates are being up-front and offer the interviewer reassurance in the form of professional references. We all go through difficult patches; what matters to an interviewer is how we deal with them. The candidates may be questioned further, but if they maintain their openness, they should find themselves giving a good impression.

GAPS IN EMPLOYMENT

UNEMPLOYMENT, REDUNDANCY AND A RETURN TO WORK

'You've been out of work for quite some time now ... '

As one leading employer said, 'The traditional stigma associated with being unemployed is not relevant today. Often it is down to the luck of the draw.' Even so, less enlightened employers treat warily people who have been unemployed for any length of time. The reassurance they need is that your skills are up to scratch, that you will be able to cope with the work routine, that your knowledge of current practices and issues is up to date.

Your answer might draw on real-life examples (non-work, obviously) to indicate relevant skills and personal qualities. If you have been, or intend to go, on a training course mention this too, and provide evidence of how you have spent the intervening time – attending government-sponsored courses, taking part in voluntary-work activities or using the time constructively to rethink your career.

If you are trying to find your first foot-hold in employment, an employer may be concerned about whether you will be able to adapt to working full-time. Think about experience which will provide reassurance, such as work-experience placements, voluntary work or regular attendance at, and involvement in, community activities. Anything which demonstrates your ability to handle responsibility will help.

If they want to know about the circumstances of a redundancy, the best way to deal with this is to place the redundancy label on the job you had, not on yourself (that is, due to reorganisation your *position* became redundant).

- ◆ When the post became redundant because of a major restructuring exercise I took the opportunity to rethink my career and eventually decided to update my skills, focus on the training aspect and move away from the supervisory role. Since then I've successfully secured a number of short-term contracts to tide me over until I found the right sort of company, one with a more progressive approach like yours. I'm really interested in your commitment to being a learning organisation.

◆ I realise it's a more competitive market now, so I've used the opportunity to complete a computer-skills course. I notice you use the same software here.

Key points   The first candidate is able to account for his time out of work relatively easily, using a number of positive-sounding words and phrases to help: 'took the opportunity', 'positive', 'successfully'. He's brought an up-beat feel to a down-beat situation. With less to dwell on, the second candidate focuses on her recent training, especially as it is directly relevant to the job, and uses it to help move the interview forward. A less effective reply would find interviewers listening to a sorrowful experience of unemployment. They may be sympathetic, but that will not convince them you could do the job.

RETURNING TO WORK

Will you be able to cope with the work-a-day routine? Are your skills adequate? Will you be able to do the job? These issues will concern the interviewer so demonstrate your skills by drawing on real life examples. If you are a parent returning to paid work after bringing up children, there are many skills that can be brought to the interviewer's attention. As Tesco remarked, 'Many returners have managed to cope with several kids, running a budget, handling catering and generally co-ordinating family life – all skills that qualify them for jobs with us.'

Questions may be phrased in many ways.

'How do you feel about returning to work after such a long break?'
◆ Great! After being away for so long, I'm really keen to get back again. I see the new legislation went through at last. I can't wait to get to grips with that.

Key points   He's been out of work but not out of touch. Not only that but he's full of enthusiasm and obviously on the ball.

'How do you think you could cope with the demands and responsibilities of a full-time job?'

◆   Although I've been raising my family, with all the organising that entails, I've spent much of my time sitting on the board of the local Health Authority in a voluntary capacity – making site visits, report-writing and attending regular panels. I've also successfully completed the new diploma for our profession. I feel more than up to handling a full-time job.

Key points   She's outlined her continuing involvement in her profession and ability to operate at a senior level, albeit in an unpaid capacity. This candidate is dynamic and asserts her confidence in her abilities, which should reassure the interviewer.

'I think you'll find things have changed quite a lot since you were last in employment.'

◆   Indeed they have. I notice that recently . . .

◆   I thought so too, so I've signed up for/completed the new course in . . .

Key points   Don't let yourself be caught out on this point. It's a golden opportunity to show that you're bang up to date with all the developments which have taken place while you've been away from the workplace.

CRIMINAL RECORDS

Whether to disclose information about convictions is not as straightforward as it may seem. Laws relating to disclosure depend on whether a conviction is 'spent', which is not simply to do with whether a sentence has been served or not. The period of time before which a conviction is officially spent varies, and any conviction over thirty months will never be spent. Unless a conviction is spent, if you are asked about a criminal record the law says you must disclose it. If you are not asked, the law does not insist you volunteer the information. If in doubt, contact the Apex Trust or NACRO, which has a useful guide called 'Disclosing Convictions' (see Appendix B).

We probably all have weak points in our employment record. We can pray they won't be noticed, but it's the interviewer's job to spot them all and satisfy any anxieties they might have. Interviewers *will* ask questions. The only way to go into an interview with confidence is to be prepared. A well thought-out response can count in your favour, so go through your application and practise replies that will enable you to handle awkward questions with confidence instead of confusion.

What are You Worth?

Out of 215 job vacancies advertised recently in a Saturday *Guardian* only 10 per cent mentioned an exact, single-figure salary. These excluded jobs in the public sector, education and other professions, where a salary scale is well established, but included jobs in the media, marketing, sales, secretarial, PR, computing and some graduate appointments. The remaining 90 per cent of the advertised vacancies gave no precise figure for the salary, and some 40 per cent quoted no figure at all.

YOUR WORTH IN THE JOB MARKET

In the adveriisements, employers handled the subject of pay in the following ways:

NO DETAILS OF PAY GIVEN

Phrases used to mask a lack of specific information about pay included 'Competitive salary', 'Good salary', 'Attractive package', 'Pay negotiable', 'Salary according to qualifications and experience', but some carried no reference to pay at all.

SOME INDICATION OF PAY

Nearly 20 per cent indicated a salary range (for example £18,500–£21,000). Over 10 per cent quoted a *circa* figure, indicating room for negotiation. Some set a ceiling figure of 'up to', while others gave a minimum figure (for example, 'minimum starting salary £12,500'). A small number gave a figure that was 'negotiable'.

PUTTING THE BALL IN THE APPLICANT'S COURT

Instead of providing an indication of salary some employers invited applicants effectively to make the first move. As part of their application they were asked to include 'details of current salary', 'present remuneration', 'salary requirements' or 'salary expectations'. This strategy automatically deselects those applicants who price themselves out of the running – and help employers snap up a bargain. A total of 10 per cent of employers chose this option.

From these figures it seems fair to assume that before you can call a job yours, salary negotiation will in all likelihood have to be entered into. Even in the public sector some jobs may have a negotiable starting-point on their pay scale. The ones which provide little room for manoeuvre are unskilled jobs and those for which a going rate is well established. If a fast-food chain wants you to serve their food to the public, they will tell you exactly what they will pay per hour. Take it or leave it.

Women in particular have much to gain from successful salary negotiation – and lots of ground to make up. The Equal Opportunities Commission pointed out that in 1996 women lagged an average 20 per cent behind men in their pay. In addition, the older a woman is, the greater the pay difference. A woman in her forties earns 25 per cent less than her male equivalent. The difference falls to 10 per cent for women in their twenties – an improvement but still outrageous when this could mean earning £100 less per month on a £12,000 salary than she should be getting. The *Guardian*'s 'Powerful People' survey in 1996 revealed that women also miss out on fringe benefits like bonuses, share options, car allowances and health insurance.

DOING THE GROUND WORK

Before salary negotiations take place it is vitally important to know the going rate for the job. Relying on one's own sense of what a job is worth is not a good (and probably not even a realistic) base to work from: it's no better than hearsay or anecdote. Only knowledge of fully current pay rates will do, taking as a guideline what a *male* employee could expect to receive. Without this information it is relatively easy for an employer to get away with paying too little.

To find out current pay rates, these sources might help:

◆ professional networking contacts – who do you know who could get some current figures for you?

◆ executive search firms, employment agencies and Job-centres

◆ professional associations

◆ trade associations or unions

◆ job advertisements which *do* quote a salary – but check they are broadly comparable in terms of location, size of organisation, level of responsibility, whether in the same sector (for example, commercial *vs* public), etc. Compare salary ranges and find an average.

PREPARATION

Before entering into negotiation, you will need more than a ball-park figure in mind to get you through. Knowing your likely worth to the employer, your negotiating aims and identifying points on which you are willing to trade are also important.

YOUR VALUE

Assess how valuable you are to the employer. Yes, they have expressed a positive interest in taking you on, but they may be equally happy to take on one of the other candidates should the salary negotiation fall through. On the other hand, you may have an outstanding track record in previous jobs or skills which are scarce in the market-place. Think about what business people refer to as your Unique Selling Points (USPs) – those things which set you apart from the rest – and take into account your age and level of experience.

Take their needs into account too. They may be a small, struggling business with not much financial slack to play around with. They may be desperate for someone to start immediately – and you might be free; if you have other positions to consider, they may offer more. They may want the contacts or sector knowledge you could bring (especially if you presently work for one of their competitors). The employer may be keen to have you rather than another candidate simply because you hit it off. Based on your knowledge of the company and the job, consider which other factors might affect your bargaining power – and which ones might affect theirs.

SALARY REQUIREMENTS

How much do you need to live on? What impact will taking the job have on your outgoings? Will you spend more on travel? Will you need to pay for child-care? Total your outgoings over the last year, including the cost of holidays and Christmas, and add any new expenses you would incur by taking the job. If you intend to use this opportunity to start a pension or savings plan, take account of this as well.

The figure you arrive at is *not* the figure to aim for in negotiations. This figure is what must go into your bank account after tax and National Insurance have been paid. If you are a standard-rate taxpayer, approximately a third of your salary goes in direct taxation. To work out the income you need, divide your total outgoings by 2, then multiply the result by 3. This figure is the minimum salary you need, and it should be at the lower end of the range which you bring to the negotiating table. If you need £20,000, a salary range could be £19,500 to £22,000. Never suggest an exact figure – it could end up being the one from which the employer negotiates downwards.

PRESENT SALARY

Work out your present salary and itemise any benefits you currently receive. These might include company car, non-contributory pension scheme, bonus scheme, subsidised mortgage, interest-free season ticket loan, free or discounted products and services, and so on. Work out the cash value of each item. Similar benefits may be attached to the new job, but if not, the impact of their loss on your income could be considerable. Calculate any savings which would be made as a result of taking the new job (for example, on travel if the workplace is closer to home).

TRADING POINTS

Although the basic salary may be nothing exceptional, the value of added benefits in the new job could make all the difference. Information about these may have been included in the details sent to applicants. If the information is to hand, work out the value of each beforehand and include it in your calculations. If no specific mention of benefits has been made, here is a list of typical ones in addition to those referred to in the previous section:

- car-related allowances

- travel pass

- free or subsidised club memberships

- expense account

- private health insurance

- profit-sharing scheme

- free sports and leisure facilities

- relocation expenses

- funding for training

- share options

- cheap loans

- subsidised staff restaurant

- clothing allowance

- luncheon vouchers

- childcare provision.

If the final offer is lower than you had hoped but you want to take the job, other trading points might include:

- agreeing on a salary increase after three or six months – a useful tactic if they have marked the salary offer down because of your lack of experience

- agreeing regular salary reviews

- agreeing to a performance-related increase (for example, if you manage to bring in a key contract within a specified period)

- negotiating an agreement to allow working at home – to reduce their office overheads and your travel costs

- negotiating a reduction in hours/days worked

- negotiating to exclude certain aspects of the job.

From what you know of the job, the company and your own financial situation, note any other points on which you would be willing to trade or negotiate.

NEGOTIATING

If the thought of negotiating a salary embarrasses, even terrifies you, try separating yourself from identifying personally with the figures under negotiation. Instead think of the salary as you would a house, needing to be dressed in a saleable package. The employer suggests new carpets would do; you look at the effect, and although it's not bad, you would like the house redecorated, too – and perhaps a new kitchen to go with it. 'I'll settle for redecoration, but the kitchen is out of my range,' says the employer. 'I could perhaps stretch to new flooring, though.' 'Quarry tiles?' you ask hopefully. 'Vinyl,' she replies. All the while both parties focus on the house, not on personalising the issue.

Thinking of the salary as a common problem under discussion not only depersonalises the matter but also sets it outside the confrontational arena. This makes it easier to avoid falling into the trap of becoming defensive or aggressive when suggestions are put forward which are not agreeable. Calm and reasoned logic (armed with facts and figures), along with a professional attitude, are what salary negotiation calls for. Personalising the discussion or showing an unwillingness to enter into the give-and-take won't help.

Clarifying your salary aims, knowing your lowest acceptable figure and understanding the value of additional benefits will allow you to participate fully in the negotiation.

STEPS TO NEGOTIATION

Money talk will take place only after they have decided on you as their first choice, so it's unlikely to happen at your initial interview; they will have other people to see and will want to take time to make their final selection. Negotiation will take place at a second meeting. They may spend time clarifying any outstanding points with you but are more likely to go straight into negotiation.

Although some employers try to make candidates put a figure on the table first, try to avoid doing so at all costs. It is generally accepted that if they do, most applicants (perhaps especially women) will give a figure far below what the employer would be willing to pay – apart from the occasional ones who seriously overestimate their real value in the market-place. If you have done your research, this should not happen.

When an employer tries to get you to name a figure, pass the ball back into their court. For example, you could say something like:

- 'Well, the job involves a fair level of responsibility, especially compared with my present one. I would expect the salary to reflect this. *What kind of figure do you have in mind?*'

- 'I appreciate this is an entry-level job, but I have good qualifications. *What sort of range were you thinking of?*'

- 'What is the company's normal salary range at this level?'

With luck they will oblige and name a figure that is at the top end of your range, if not above it. If this doesn't happen and they insist on a figure from you, state the range you have worked out beforehand.

When an employer insists on pinning you down on present salary, keep the figure slightly vague ('Over £15,000'), but gently remind them of the differences between the two positions which contribute to the case for a higher figure, such as more responsibility. Say something like 'And so I am looking for a figure which reflects this.'

Once the initial offer is on the table, judge whether it is reasonable and start off negotiations if it isn't: 'What room for manoeuvre is there on that figure?' If they reply that there isn't any, you could accept and go on to ask about what benefits they can offer; or you could ignore them and open up the negotiation with 'What about another £1,000 on that figure?' or 'I'd like to see a figure more like £20,000.'

On the other hand, if they keep the discussion open but pass the ball back by asking what figure you had in mind, quote a *range* – not necessarily the one you worked out at home but one which puts their offer towards the bottom of a (new) range, giving them room to manoeuvre further upwards. For example, if their offer was 'somewhere in the region of £16,000', your response might be something like 'I had a figure of between £15,500 and £17,000 and was looking towards the top end of that. Could you improve on your offer?' Even if you had originally been hoping for £15,000 at best, go for what you can reasonably get – but don't push so hard that you merely seem greedy. Successful negotiations happen when both parties maintain respect for each other throughout.

Once the basic salary figure is established, go on to ask about additional benefits. Make a note of them. See how they compare with your present entitlements. If they do not include one which you currently enjoy, or one which you hoped would be offered, ask if it could be included in the offer.

If the calculations and comparisons look too difficult to make there and then, or if you have other offers to compare with this one, you could say that you would like time to consider the offer and agree when you will contact them. If the offer fulfils expectations, check that it is their final offer (they may have a trump card up their sleeve). Accept graciously when you are satisfied with what is on the table.

Of course, sometimes the final offer isn't right. In this case, you take the job because of its long-term prospects or because it is your dream job and you'd probably do it for nothing anyway; negotiate around the job itself (see page 119); or decide to decline the offer. There is a possibility they may come back with a final, revised offer if you do decline, but if they don't and the pay just isn't good enough, there is nothing much else to do. And if they can't afford to pay what you know you are worth in the market-place, perhaps this indicates something about the job or the company.

If the notion of negotiating still feels uncomfortable, practice will undoubtedly help. Even starting to haggle with market traders will help you to get over the psychological hurdle of entering into negotiations over money. Once over it, some people negotiate as a matter of course.

A lot hangs on how assertively you handle the discussion. Put embarrassment aside. If someone is willing to pay you an extra, say, £2,000 every year, it makes sense to put up with a few minutes' discomfort while negotiations get under way.

Decisions, Decisions

'Many are called, but few are chosen.' The Bible could have been referring to job interviews instead of wedding guests. The fact is that out of all who apply, and out of all who are interviewed, only one can possibly be chosen to fill each vacancy. The final part of the interview process, when this choosing takes place, has not one but two aspects: employers make their decision about who to make the job offer to, and the successful applicant has to decide whether to accept.

THEIR DECISION

From the employer's point of view, the decision may be easy. If all but one outstanding candidate failed to meet the criteria for the job, the choice will be relatively straightforward and quickly made. On the other hand, if there is little to choose between candidates, the task becomes much more involved. Lone interviewers face the difficulty of having no one to compare notes with, unlike members of an interviewing panel.

Knowing what employers take into consideration and how they reach a decision can be helpful, especially if a job offer doesn't come our way. Otherwise it is tempting to take a rejection personally – which is neither helpful nor, in all likelihood, appropriate. Of course, there are times, especially in one-to-one interviews, when two people just don't hit it off: this can happen as readily as instant rapport. All we can do is try not to be fazed and continue to give as good an interview as possible. One of the aims of an interview is to allow both parties to see what they would be letting themselves in for. It's not a question simply of whether we match an employer's explicit criteria; there is also the consideration about fitting in well with the organisation and other staff.

If the interview did not go well because of a lack of rapport, a thanks-but-no-thanks letter will still be disappointing – no one enjoys rejection – but at least understandable. To accept the interviewer's decision easily when an interview seems to have gone reasonably smoothly is more difficult. The decision can leave us feeling angry and confused: 'What did I do wrong?' 'I don't believe it!' 'But I thought it went really well.'

Some employers are willing to debrief applicants which can help enormously. With luck, they will explain why they reached the decision and perhaps offer some constructive advice. If there is a specific point on which you would like feedback, ask.

To reach a decision about who will receive the job offer, interviewers look at:

- which candidate could best demonstrate an ability to carry out the duties, as outlined in the job description

- which candidate appeared to match the person specification most closely

- which candidate had the most appropriate level of knowledge, experience and/or skills necessary in order to be effective in the job

- information provided on application forms, such as which candidate had the best qualifications

- additional information revealed or volunteered by each candidate at interview

- the importance or relevance of any 'negative' aspects of each candidate which may have come to light at interview

- which candidate would provide the best degree of organisational fit

- results of psychometric tests

- which candidate gave the best overall impression, including level of motivation, enthusiasm and likely commitment to the job and company.

If a panel is making the decision, the members' observations (which may not necessarily concur) have to be considered and balanced, the process normally being governed by the panel chair. All interviewers will also take into account pressure to make an appointment from the field of candidates seen. Time and money may not be on their side.

Unless there is an outstanding candidate, it is easy to see how the task before interviewers can prove quite daunting. The ostensibly simple job of choosing the most suitable applicant can turn into a complex problem. What often becomes apparent is that each candidate excels in some areas but shows weakness in others. This is what makes an interviewer's job difficult.

As a result of weighing up the pros and cons, one of the following courses of action is decided upon:

- a candidate is selected

- a further interview or, possibly, a work trial is arranged with a candidate if doubts linger over the final choice

- no candidate is selected and the position is re-advertised.

If a job offer does not come your way, try not to be too dismayed or start to worry about the quality of your performance. Unless you accept that you failed to do yourself justice or feedback from the interviewers suggests this, reassure yourself that the final decision may have come down to the fact that, all candidates being equally good, only one person could be chosen. Unfortunately, this time it was someone else. It is also worth remembering that interviewers are not infallible and wrong choices are made.

YOUR DECISION

This part is easy if the job is what you have always wanted and you liked what you saw at interview. But life isn't always that simple, and just as employers can have a tough time assessing candidates, it can be equally difficult for a successful applicant to reach a decision. The matter may be far from cut and dried. And a job which sounded great in an advertisement may look very different by the time the end of the selection process has been reached.

Outside pressures, which have nothing to do with the attractiveness of the job as such, can play a major role in deciding whether or not to accept. Considerations may be:

◆ financial pressures – the debts are mounting and savings receding

◆ the present job – is it really that awful? What about transferring to a new department/section/branch or putting in a request for training which would help with promotion? Would an assertiveness or conflict-resolution skills course solve the problem of interpersonal difficulties? Would asking for a salary increase help?

◆ the length of time unemployed – this is the first job offer in a *long* time. You have a personal need to be in work; accepting will help reactivate the CV

◆ family pressures – *they* all think it's great, but do you?

◆ a partner's ambitions – they may be more ambitious for your career than you are

◆ how keen a partner is to relocate – potentially a major problem if the job is abroad

◆ income requirements – the new job sounds great but will it pay the bills?

◆ the likelihood of another suitable vacancy arising – is this job probably all that will be on offer for the foreseeable future?

Many other factors are likely to come into play, some major, some trivial, depending on individual circumstances. The decision may even end up swinging in favour of accepting for no more important a reason than because your present car is on its last legs and a new company car would be a boon.

Linked to an array of personal considerations are ones that relate directly to the job and company. Through research, pre-interview visits and the interview itself the reality of a job becomes clearer, yet it may raise doubts which weren't there before. This can make reaching a decision far from easy.

New thoughts about the job might include:

◆ the job itself. The emphasis given at interview on particular aspects of the job may have put a different slant on it. What it actually entails could be different from what was imagined. The level of responsibility may be different too. Perhaps your understanding of what could be required in the job has changed

◆ the working conditions. These could make a big difference to the attractiveness of a job. The dingy corner which would be your workplace could decide you against accepting. Conversely, a bright modern workplace which makes a job seem attractive, which can simply cloud the issue

◆ the people. The job may be fine, but what about the people who would be your colleagues, line manager, supervisor or boss? What about the clientele, customers, outside contractors and any others with whom you would have regular contact? They may not have struck you as potential friends, but did you feel you could work productively alongside them? Did you sense any undercurrents? Has the prospect of a new job made you feel differently about losing current colleagues? If so, how important is this?

♦ the company. Each business has its own culture. In a small enterprise this can be much affected by the owner's personality. In larger businesses the company culture is often more market-driven. The question in either case is whether you like the feel of the place, whether you feel you would happily fit in. Is the company stable? At interview were any statements made about the company and its future which conflicted with facts gleaned through your research? Did they hint at any major changes in the near future? How strong did the management appear to be? Did it look like a professionally run operation?

♦ the location. If the interview provided the only opportunity to visit the company, what was the journey like? Could you envisage doing it every day? If the job would entail a major relocation, what about the area? Perhaps you need more time to decide if you and your family would be happy there

♦ the prospects. It may have seemed that the job would open new doors but, after the interview, are those the doors you want to go through? Was talk of promotion substantiated or was it just flannel? What was revealed about training provision? How secure is the job?

♦ changes the job would bring. A new job means change in itself, but it can also necessitate other changes which impact on life outside work: childcare arrangements; overall lifestyle and social life; hours worked; where you live; schooling arrangements; working patterns; travel arrangements; time spent away from home; degree of stress.

When the issue is not clear-cut, it's well worth giving yourself enough time to think it through carefully, and discussing it with partners, family members and friends who are capable of being objective. They may come up with suggestions or new angles which clarify the issue.

A decision has to be reached, but when advantages and disadvantages balance, what can be done? One suggestion is to make a decision to accept the offer but not to act on the decision immediately. Instead live with the idea of working in the job. Act as if you were going to hand in your notice and start working for your new employers at the beginning of next month. Make mental adjustments to accommodate any changes which surface in the wake of your decision. Tell one or two friends (not colleagues) of your decision. Live for as long as possible with the idea of taking the job, even if there is only an afternoon in which to do it. It's like trying on a pair of shoes before buying. Walk around in the prospect for a while and see how it feels. Then make your final decision.

THE FORMAL JOB OFFER

When you hear the job is yours, do nothing about handing in your notice until a formal offer is received in writing. Jobs, management, funding can disappear almost literally overnight, and if you hand in your notice prematurely, you could be stranded. Cover your back and wait until the formal job offer has been received and any contracts of employment signed.

A formal job offer should include:

◆ the terms and conditions of employment, including things like holidays, sick pay, hours to be worked, length of any probationary period, period of notice, salary, benefits, etc. Carefully check over these and make sure they comply with what was agreed at interview. Mistakes can and do happen

◆ specific conditions which apply to the job offer, such as satisfactory references, medical reports, verification of other relevant information

- an agreed start date.

The job offer should also indicate how you in turn should respond and by what date. Sometimes a signature on duplicate documents is all that is required; at other times, you will need to write a letter of acceptance.

LETTERS OF ACCEPTANCE

A letter of acceptance need not be wordy. Something along these lines will suffice:

> I am writing to thank you for the offer of the post of Senior Marketing Manager which I received today. I am delighted to accept.

> I confirm I will be able to start work at the beginning of April, as specified.

> I would like to take the opportunity to say how much I am looking forward to joining Jones & Co. and the new marketing team. I hope we will both enjoy a successful future working together.

Flavour it with your own words and include any specific confirmations requested by the employer in their job offer.

DECLINING A JOB OFFER

A letter to decline a job offer need not be wordy either. Something along these lines will suffice:

> I am writing to thank you for the offer of the post of Senior Marketing Manager. After careful consideration I have decided to decline.

> I would like to take the opportunity to thank you for taking such a keen interest in my application and wish Jones & Co. every success in the future.

If you want to keep your options open for the future, perhaps because the job was not quite right but the company was, you might want to include something like:

> Although I felt this particular post was not quite right for me, I would like to be considered in the future for any positions of a more sales-oriented nature which arise.

Again, use words and phrases to personalise it your own way.

RESIGNING FROM A JOB

Do I have to bother putting my resignation in writing? Yes, even if you tell your present employer in person. It is a good idea to have the letter already prepared, and to hand it over as you inform them. This oils the wheels of the interaction.

The letter doesn't have to go into great detail about your reasons for leaving unless you particularly want it to:

> I am writing to confirm my resignation from the post of Junior Marketing Manager, with effect from the end of this month. I shall be taking up a new position as from 1 April.
>
> I would like to take the opportunity to say how much I have enjoyed my time here at Ace Ltd. The experience I have gained has been invaluable and I fully appreciate the company's support and professional input over the years.
>
> I wish everyone here at Ace continuing success in the future.

And when this final procedure is complete, you can look forward to popping the corks in celebration of your interview success. Congratulations!

Appendix A
Further Reading

Body language

The Secret Language of Success, Dr David Lewis (Corgi, 1990)

Communication skills

Improve Your Communication Skills, Malcolm Peel, 2nd edn (Kogan Page, 1995)

Say What You Mean and Get What You Want, George R. Walther (Piatkus, 1993)

Your Voice, Andrew Armitage (Right Way Books, 1992)

Company research

Kelly's Business Directory

Key British Enterprises (Dun and Bradstreet)

UK Kompass Register

Who Owns Whom (Dun and Bradstreet)

Confidence

Total Confidence: The Complete Guide to Self-Assurance and Personal Success, Philippa Davies (Piatkus, 1995)

General

101 Ways to Make a Professional Impact, Eleri Sampson (Kogan Page, 1996)

Negotiation

Never Take No for an Answer: A Guide to Successful Negotiation, Samfrits Le Poole, 2nd edn (Kogan Page, 1991)

Presentation skills

Colour Me Beautiful, Carole Jackson (Piatkus, 1995)

The Image Factor, Eleri Sampson (Kogan Page, 1996)

Presenting Yourself: A Personal Image Guide for Men, Mary Spillane (Piatkus, 1994)

Presenting Yourself: A Personal Image Guide for Women, Mary Spillane (Piatkus, 1994)

Psychometric testing

How to Pass Graduate Recruitment Tests, Mike Bryon (Kogan Page, 1994)

How to Succeed in Psychometric Tests, David Cohen (Sheldon Press, 1993)

Test Your Own Aptitude, Jim Barrett and Geoff Williams, 2nd edn (Kogan Page, 1990)

Stress

Creative Visualization, Shakti Gawain (Bantam, 1987)

Stress Control Through Self-Hypnosis, Dr Arthur Jackson (Piatkus, 1993)

Appendix B
Useful Addresses

APEX Trust, St Alphage House, Wingate Annexe, 2 Fore Street, London EC2Y 5DA; tel. 0171-638 5931. Help, advice and support for ex-offenders.

Commission for Racial Equality, Elliot House, 10–12 Allington Street, London SW1E 5EH; tel. 0171-828 7022. *Or* Hanover House, 45–51 Hanover Street, Edinburgh EH2 2PJ; tel. 0131-226 5186. For help and advice if you think you have been unfairly discriminated against on racial grounds.

Equal Opportunities Commission, Overseas House, Quay Street, Manchester M3 3NN; tel. 0161-833 9244. *Or* Stock Exchange House, 7 Nelson Mandela Place, Glasgow G2 1NQ; tel. 0141-248 5833. *Or* Caerwys House, Windsor Lane, Cardiff CF1 1LB; tel. 01222 343552. For help and advice if you think you have been unfairly discriminated against on grounds of sex, race or disability.

NACRO – National Association for the Care and Resettlement of Offenders, 169 Clapham Road, London SW9 0PU; tel. 0171-582 6500. Help, advice and support for ex-offenders.